LEE HO!

" *The love that is given to ships is profoundly different from the love men feel for every other work of their hands...*"

Joseph Conrad
'*The Mirror of the Sea*' 1906

Written and Illustrated by Leo Harris

Published by
Channel Island Publishing
Unit 3b, Barette Commercial Centre
La Route du Mont Mado
St John, Jersey JE3 4DS

Copyright © Leo Harris 2008
All rights reserved. No part of this publication may
be reproduced, stored in a retrieval system, or transmitted, in any form or
by any means without the prior written permission of the publishers.

Cover design: Alison Richards from an oil painting,
'Bay Racing' by Leo Harris

Printed by Cromwell Press, Trowbridge, Wiltshire

ISBN 978-1-905095-19-8

Publisher's Note

Every effort has been made to trace copyright of material in
chapter 2 and the author and theImperial War Museum would
be grateful for any information which might help to trace those
whose identities or addresses are not currently known.

LEE HO!

50 Years
Sailing Around
The Channel Islands

Leo Harris

Acknowledgments

I could not have started this book without the frequent company of many friends in the sailing world. Their 'yarns' and personal experiences have been drawn on heavily and I thank them all and ask them to forgive my omissions, corruption of their stories and generally 'getting it all wrong'.

Among this company I would like to thank, Kevin Le Scelleur for allowing me to delve into his 'The Evacuation of St Malo' and for introducing me to 'B.E.F. Ships' by his friend John de S. Winser. Also Don Filleul, Gordon Coombs, Bill Morvan, Don Thompson, David and Micky Nicolle, Jurat Roy Bullen, Graham Talbot and Margaret, John Chevalier and Sue, Harry Fenn, Dudley Harrison, Sheila Jones, Brian Slous. M Bertrand, Terry Ashborn and Pamela, Fred Daly and the other members of the St Helier Yacht Club Coffee Club. The list is endless and I apologize to all those I have forgotten to mention whose input over the years has inspired this book.

I also wish to acknowledge the assistance given to me by the Trustees of the Imperial War Museum and the Departments of Documents and Photography at the Museum for allowing access to the papers of Major JFJ Rex. In particular I would like to thank Yvonne Oliver and Sabrina Rowlatt. Also the Librarians of the States of Jersey who deserve praise for their skill and interest.

My own family, beginning with Yvonne, have also encouraged me and have read and read again and listened to chapter after chapter. Yvonne, of course, was my frequent sailing companion from the 50's onward and we still sail on. Alison has put much work and thought into this book especially the cover design, while Frances has contributed in a similar way providing much input for the illustrations. I am fortunate in having them around me. I will not forget to mention my brother Francis too who introduced me to sailing.

Finally my publishers have been most helpful and understanding of my requirements and their professional approach has often made what was difficult appear to be quite easy. Thank you Chris, Simon and Lee.

Contents

Foreword	8
Introduction	9
St Helier Yacht Club	15
The Little Dunkirk	22
Falcons Galore	41
It Pays To Take Care	55
A Tragedy Of Mishaps	67
Jonquil	78
The Gaffers	91
The Marguerite	100
Remember, It's Only A Bit of Wire	105
The 'Compleat Yachtsman'	113
September Tide	125
Lalun	130
Chausey	144
Dancing Lady	151
Granville	159
Blue Raven	174
The Moorings	189
On Leaving Your Yacht	199
Splash And Splot	205
Canals And Rivers	213
Glossary	235
About the author	239

Foreword

W.J. Morvan is a noted Jersey politician, former Senator of the States of Jersey, Connetable of the Parish of St Lawrence, President of the Harbours and Airport Committee and an outstanding yachtsman, at one time Commodore of St Helier Yacht Club.

This is the third book written by Leo Harris that I have read. The first two were of his experiences during the German Occupation of Jersey. This is different, it covers a much longer period of time, in fact since the war to about the turn of the twentieth century.

In this book the author touches on many subjects, interesting, likable, brave and sometimes foolish people come to life in his writing; boats he and his wife Yvonne owned, sailed and raced, places they have visited and enjoyed; and a lot more.

Finally, it is a good and interesting read and it seems to me that we have shared hobbies though I envy him his woodworking and writing abilities.

W.J. Morvan
10th September 2008

Introduction

"I know you can take your time sailing about, but I think you would have got round faster than that," my daughter, Alison said on reading the title of this book. Well, it's just a title to a book and I did start sailing in 1956 and it is now 2008, so I felt that I could be said to have fifty years experience of Channel Island waters. It would have been longer, but I was waylaid into golf for several years, in fact since 1952. Two friends and I had become members of La Moye Golf Club when the Clubhouse was a wooden pavilion to grace it with a better name than it deserved. I was never a good player, but I enjoyed the company, the fresh air and the stunning views across St Ouen's Bay to the sea. I will not say that the sea was calling me, it never did, but I have crossed and recrossed that stretch of water many times since.

My brother Francis, more than two years my senior, did not play golf and singularly failed to understand its attraction. Terry Ashborn was a friend of Francis and he was into all sorts of watersports including sailing and canoeing. One of Terry's possessions was a neat, clinker wooden dinghy of about eight feet in length. 'Water Rat' was heavily built and sported a short mast and a small mainsail. It was the summer of 1956 when Francis offered me a sail round St Helier harbour in 'Water Rat'. Terry had been showing Francis how to sail and I think Francis now needed a crew to sail her, for Terry had offered him the occasional use of his little craft. I needed no second invitation.

It was not our first venture under sail. In 1947 my father, who was definitely not a sailor, had bought us two boys a little carvel hulled dinghy of about six feet in length. The idea was that we should row it off La Rocque where we were then living. Rowing soon palled and an early 'Harris' attempt to fit it with a very temperamental, ex lawnmower, inboard motor had been a complete failure, one of the worst 'do-it-yourself' jobs you could imagine. Now we decided that sail was the thing.

We 'rigged' a short mast and fitted to it a square sail made out of blue oilcloth salvaged from an old roller blind and set forth from our beach at La Rocque with a stiff following breeze. Steering with an oar, we made rapid, if not very steady progress for about half-an-hour towards the outer reefs and the open sea.

On closer inspection the sea looked very rough with quite sizeable waves and the occasional white crest tossing its head. Discretion now overcame valour and we moved our steering oar to 'come about', or some other sort of jolly, nautical parlance. Alas, only then did we realize that our square sail, while well suited to running before the wind, had very real shortcomings when you wanted to sail directly into the wind where lay the beach of our earlier departure.

We shipped water, we dropped our sail, we almost capsized, we bailed out and then we noticed that something was carrying us fast towards the nearby rocks. We grabbed our oars and struck out as strongly as we could for the beach. I was seventeen and Francis was nearly

Introduction

twenty so with youthful energy and much hard work we reached the beach, a good deal shocked and very far from our launching site.

As we stood, soaked to the skin, catching our breath alongside our little craft, a gentleman came quickly towards us across the wet beach and clearly told us how stupid we had been. He had watched our 'goings on' and had now come from his house to give us the benefit of his experience. He was, of course, entirely right.

So it was that I found myself in 'Water Rat' careering up and down in the confines of a very quiet harbour with very few moorings in any part of it. The tough little craft was quite responsive and sailed well. I clambered about at my brother's bidding while he enjoyed this increase to his power and authority over me. Something stirred and woke up within me, I loved sailing!

Later, I was to meet in the nearby St Helier Yacht Club Squadron Leader Tony Messiter R.A.F (Ret'd). Tony was a former fighter pilot of the 1920's and had flown in all sorts of climes, Persia, Iraq, India as well as at home in England. His talk was of 'Gamecocks' and 'Bristol Bulldogs' and the other lovely old biplanes of that era and of course lovely yarns about life as a young officer in the Middle East.

At an early stage in his career, on arriving at an R.A.F Station in Persia he had 'inherited' from the officer he was replacing, an enormous American open touring car of early vintage complete with native driver. Apparently the driver only needed half-an-hour's notice to prepare the vehicle for duty. This ceremonial included opening the long, heavy bonnet giving access to the eight cylinder engine and then removing all the spark plugs. A nearby gutter was then dammed with clay and liberally flooded with petrol. The plugs were set in a row along the edge of the pavement with their points over the petrol lake which was then lit! When the flames had finally subsided, the plugs, now roasting hot, were manhandled back into place and the engine cranked into life by means of a massive starting handle protruding from just below the radiator between the front dumb irons.

This grand old vehicle would then arrive to pick up its proud owner and friends who would settle themselves in the rear accommodation while their chauffeur conducted them through the local 'traffic' of donkeys, camels and pedestrians with much swerving and blowing of a great air horn.

On occasion a fuel starvation problem would develop and was quickly solved by hiring a local boy to lie on the inside of the front mudguard alongside the engine with the bonnet tied open to facilitate the feeding of petrol into the carburettor bowl by means of a handheld tin can. Tony had parted with this fine old car after descending a steep incline on a dust road in the mountains. A large car wheel had suddenly appeared from somewhere behind him and had sped downhill to plunge over the unguarded edge of the road and disappear into a deep ravine. He was soon made aware by more than usually erratic driving that it was his own car's rear wheel.

I liked Tony and he, on hearing that I had enjoyed my first sail, invited me to come out with him the following day aboard 'Ariel'. 'Ariel' was his pride and joy, a very pretty little, white

Introduction

yacht of just over twenty feet overall. She had a small cabin and a single mast; she was, of course, of wooden construction, built in the Edwardian period, a sloop and a pleasure to sail. I can barely describe my delight in the speed and silence of 'Ariel'. She was willing and quick to respond. I was enthralled.

Tony made sure to show her off to her best advantage and gave me the helm together with plenty of good instruction. For those who have never sailed before, sailing is such an awakening. The movement of the yacht almost like a live creature, the open sea as a space in which to manoeuvre, the entry into unusual creeks and bays, difficult to achieve by any other means, everything about it is so appealing. The names and terminology, counter, jib, sheets and halliards, 'ready about' and of course the rich tradition, which you never cease to learn. Utterly captivating.

I sold my golf clubs forthwith and never played golf again. Soon Francis purchased a 'Falcon' dinghy named 'Redshank' and I crewed for him. It was bliss!

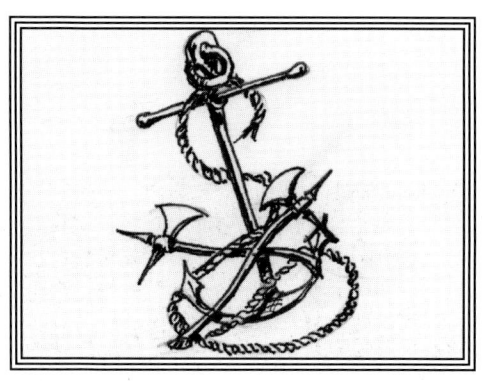

ST HELIER YACHT CLUB

You either love the sea or you would rather not know about it. I have never flown a glider, but I imagine that flying almost silently through the air, able to move effortlessly through a beautiful environment is as close as you can get to finding a comparison to handling a small yacht. There are, however, advantages to yachting. You can sail and float effortlessly for hour after hour even for extended periods of time, eat and sleep and sometimes arrive at an interesting destination, all in the company of good friends if you so wish. There is much to do, mostly light work and enjoyable such as trimming the sails, checking your position on a chart or electronic plotter, conning your little craft into or through an anchorage. Most of all it attracts a rich variety of characters, both men and women.

So it is with a good yacht club. There in a club, are gathered together yachtsmen sharing a love of the sea and a great deal of experience of its moods. Some may own a small boat, perhaps not of any great value, while the scale goes across to those who own a large and expensive craft. In my experience they are all much the same at heart, sharing a common passion for the sea.

Such a club is St Helier Yacht Club in the beautiful island of Jersey. It is here that I have encountered wonderful companionship, often married with a competitive spirit. The club began with just a few members in 1903 and has steadily grown to more than three thousand members. Not all sail, some members just enjoy the ambience of such a club, positioned as it is in the very heart of the harbour, while most share an interest in the sea aboard all types of yachts both, sail and motor.

Among its members and in common with many British Yacht clubs, you will find people from all walks of life. Lifeboat men and their coxswains, ex-sailors from the Royal Navy and our fine Merchant Service, bankers, doctors, teachers, business people, hoteliers and working men and women all bringing together a multitude of skills, knowledge and experience. This blend produces an active and living pool of good judgment and, of course, a fund of stories, most of which are true, while others are helped along by a fertile imagination, a traditional attribute of the 'ancient mariner'.

In the fifties, I had a long chat one evening in the club lounge with a tall, elderly gentleman who was a 'Cape Horner', having sailed round that Cape several times in three masted ships under canvas. I still recall his vivid description of how they fought against adverse gales of wind to round the Horn, knowing that if they failed, they would have to try again another day in perhaps worse conditions. He told me too of sheltering at anchor in bays off the south east coast of South America at Tierra del Fuego while making repairs to masts and sails; sending carpenters aloft to tighten the fids or wedges which held the upper sections of the masts securely in place. The violent working of the ship in the great seas often loosening these fids which held three separate sections of a mast together. Their loss providing a real possibility of mast, yardarms and sails falling to the deck and into the sea, together with hundreds of feet of variously sized rigging and halliards. Repairs completed, they then weighed anchor and set out to the south and to the west to try again, perhaps for several days until that blissful hour when they found themselves out into the Pacific Ocean. It was an exhausting time when the master and his crew had to drive their ship remorselessly on, taking advantage of favourable storms and 'beating' up and down across unfavourable ones. What courage and what determination.

Then there was Reg Nicolle, a true Jerseyman, a lifeboatman and physical education instructor, regaling me in deep, sonorous tones of the rescue of the 'Maurice Georges', a small French yacht which had become encircled by the reefs to the south east of Jersey one stormy night. How the coxswain of the old 'Howard D', returning from a fruitless all night search off the Normandy coast for a missing light aircraft, had received a radio message to go the aid of a small yacht and had found her. He may well have found her, but to approach her to take off her crew was well nigh an impossibility. The lifeboat and her crew were on the seaward side of a great reef over which the seas were breaking and they could discern the lights of the French yacht on the other side with no passage through to them.

Reg went on in measured phrases and with careful thought to recall how the gallant little coxswain, for Tommy King was a small man, had run the 'Howard D' back and forth parallel to the reef and had closed in, studying the situation. He had watched the white foam of the breakers as they had crashed over a great rock, well-known to him. At last he had made up his mind and ordered all his crew to lie down on the deck outside of the shelter of the minimal cockpit and its protection. "Then," declaimed Reg, "he ran her back out from that great whale back of a rock which stood before us and then turned to face it. Timing his run in, he opened wide the throttle of the single engine and surfed the 'Howard D' towards the waiting rock, which we could only see by the whiteness of the foam and spray which surrounded and washed over it. We rose mightily and surged over the great granite rock with the keel scraping the limpets and barnacles off its grim face as the craft did more than its designer in his wildest dreams had thought it would be called upon to do! We fell into a confusion of surf and boiling sea on the other side amid the thundering cascade. Tommy steered us alongside the 'Maurice Georges' and giving her a line, towed her around in circles until with dawn lightening the sky and better conditions of wind and tide combined an exit was possible."

All this, not from a book or a secondhand account, but from a great storyteller and strong character. Yet Reg could turn to assist the youngest boys and girls in the club and run a Cadet Section where they learned to row and to sail and most of all, to respect the sea; all under his careful guidance. Quite a few of the present members owe their introduction to the ways of the sea to Reg Nicolle. Yvonne, my wife, was one of those cadets and still recalls with excitement her time among them.

I never tire of hearing her tell of the time when as a girl of fourteen or thereabouts she waited in the little club 'Cadet' sailing dinghy for instructions from Reg. But he had been called away to other things and, ever the impatient girl, Yvonne had 'taken off' and sailed her little charge out of the harbour and round a warship anchored in St Aubin's Bay before returning an hour or two later to the club. Ted Larbalestier, who shared responsibility for the cadets with Reg, had caught up with Yvonne and was giving her a good telling off for her adventure while Reg hovered nearby. As Yvonne walked crestfallen away, Reg put his hand on her shoulder and said, "Mr. Larbalestier is quite right, but well done, you showed some pluck!"

I loved his 'throw away' pearls of advice. For instance, "Remember that tides don't just go up and down, they go sideways FAST." His fine Jersey-built fishing boat, 'Fiona' is now carefully kept and used by the wonderful Jersey Maritime Museum, but, alas, Reg is no longer with us to skipper her.

No one could paint a picture of such events in words as dramatically as could Reg. In his Breton cap and yellow oilskins he was the very epitome of the strong, weatherbeaten lifeboatman. As such he was noticed and photographed by Sam Sennett a leading Island photographer of his day.

Tommy King received the highest Royal National Lifeboat Institution award for the rescue of the 'Maurice Georges'. You may have guessed that he ordered his crew to lie down on the side decks before his gallant run in so that they would have had some small chance of getting clear of the lifeboat had she foundered on the rock. The South Pier of St Helier Harbour and St Helier Yacht Club, was awash with such characters and I was privileged to meet and listen to them.

A very long book would be required to cover some portion of the rich treasures of the lore of St Helier Yacht Club, but I hope to touch on at least some part of it in the pages which follow.

St Helier Yacht Club

THE LITTLE DUNKIRK

When war was declared on Germany in September 1939, a large British Expeditionary Force was sent to northern France under treaties signed with France and other countries to assist the French armed forces to repel the Germans. Unfortunately, as we know this was not sufficient and in June 1940 matters had come to a pretty pass with the gallant little army, aided by their French ally squeezed up to the Channel coast. The German 'Blitzkrieg' was unstoppable and the main French forces, although putting up a good fight, retreated and collapsed.

We also know all about the wonderful effort at Dunkirk when more than 309,000 British and allied servicemen were brought off in 'Operation Dynamo' by the Royal Navy and elements of the Merchant Service. We know of the tremendous losses in men and materiel and not least, of the brave little 'armada' of every kind of small boat whether it be yacht or fishing boat. What is not so well known, is the 'Little Dunkirk' about which I intend to tell you.

With the war in France going badly for the British and French forces in June 1940, Churchill decided early in that month to send a second British Expeditionary Force to northwestern France. On the 13th June, they were deployed by sea to Cherbourg and St Malo and amounted to 14,500 men and light equipment. A French source seems to say that it was as many as 21,000 men. The plan was to send them down to Rennes where retreating French units could form up on them. They would come up against the German Army by driving northwards and gather up more remnants of the French army on the way.

This second BEF dug in on arrival at Rennes racecourse and set up supply dumps. They then waited for orders and waited, but none came. French people came to ask them about the present position of the Germans, but they could not help them. Major Groves, one of the officers in charge of the force, records how they waited for some news of regrouping French Forces or an order to move forward, but they were held where they stood.

A Major J F Rex recorded, 'Any military order for us didn't exist. We were waiting a general evacuation order from the Garrison Commander....Today, masses of people were wandering aimlessly everywhere. They were turning this quiet town of Brittany into the atmosphere of a crowded but joyless funfair' Later on, 'A sleepless night, and during the morning the general evacuation order was issued for all troops, British and French. It was 'sauve qui peut' and we jumped on a train, which was going as far as St Malo. ENGLAND....this was the only word hammering on our thoughts now'.

After three days, they had at last received an order, 'Sauve qui Peut' which literally meant move out fast and save what you can of your force. They abandoned the majority of their supplies and all heavier equipment and took off immediately for St Malo in the hope that the British Navy would pull them out. Many soldiers marched to the railway station at Rennes and boarded cattle trucks laid on for them to travel under the cover of darkness. The rest used their motor transport. Of course, thousands of refugees had the same idea and the roads and rail links towards St Malo and other Breton ports were blocked. The troops described how trains arrived from other areas of France with refugees swarming all over the locomotive and even lying flat on the roofs of the carriages. You will now understand a little of the atmosphere which was building up in Brittany with the pressure of the advancing German army.

With the men at their disposal, men who were quite anxious to escape almost certain imprisonment for the duration of the war, they found great difficulty in clearing the roads and to assist their escape they restricted all roads to military traffic. This was not well received by the French, but it was important to retrieve the BEF if at all possible. One English refugee motorist records how he and his wife were repeatedly diverted away from their target port of St Malo until at last he acquired some paperwork from the military and reached his destination. Even then they were at first denied access to the ships, but got away eventually due to his wife's determination and persistence.

As the troops at last entered the streets of St Malo, the populace came out to cheer them, believing that they had come to make a stand against the fast approaching German Army. They mustered on the racecourse on the outskirts of the town and there they waited for their orders to proceed to the dock area. It was like a vast military jumble sale with every sort of equipment lying in disarray around this huge area. Do it yourself destruction of war materiel was attempted even to the extent of driving vehicles about until their fuel tanks ran dry. Those ordered to the docks even abandoned their knapsacks, carrying only light weapons and ammunition.

Among all this confusion some things still ran to order, a cookhouse was set up and soldiers found food and drink available. A ready source of good meat became available too as whole oxen had been laid out alongside the busy cookhouse for soldiers to help themselves. F Warner of the 88th company, Pioneer Corps who had been brought up in Hamburg in the 1920's and 30's had emigrated to England in 1939 and having enlisted into the Pioneer Corps writes descriptively about these days. He now found himself in this huge melee where cigarettes were being given away to the troops in abundance. Does it not somehow illuminate this strange disaster for our soldiers that he found time to stuff his trousers with cigarettes in the hope of taking them to England. The cigarettes did arrive at their destination held in place by his puttees, but by then they were unfit for human consumption!

Other soldiers were rifling through supplies looking for new pieces of uniform and other equipment, while a Latvian national serving with Warner stripped down a machinegun and disposed of the parts around his body. The gun caused quite a stir when it was revealed on the parade ground later at the Illfracombe Depot.

When the local inhabitants found that the British soldiers were heading for the dock area and eventual evacuation to England, they began spitting on them and shouting for them to stand and fight. However, with no formal support from the regular French Army, this was wishful thinking, and a strategic withdrawal was all that could be achieved. They arrived at the quayside on St Malo harbour and were joined all the while by stragglers, both British and French, who had escaped Dunkirk, Paris and other parts of France, swept on by the rapidly advancing Wehrmacht. The 'Blitzkrieg' had driven all before it and left the British and French Forces ineffectual and in disarray. Meanwhile the townspeople went to the racecourse and helped themselves to everything they could carry away. It is said that the Germans later made house to house searches collecting up much of these 'spoils of war'.

It was at about this time that the Admiralty swung into action and a Commander Howard-Johnston was given orders to organize the evacuation of elements of British and some French Forces out of St Malo and to destroy the new lock gates pumping stations and associated controls together with any other shiphandling equipment. He was a Naval officer of the very best tradition able to think clearly and decisively and to take action at once. He sailed from Portsmouth on Sunday the 14th of June at 2pm for Jersey aboard the destroyer H.M.S. Wild Swan accompanied by a demolition expert in a team of thirty-two men and with eight tons of explosives. 'Wild Swan' was fresh from operations at Dunkirk and Boulogne, engaging German tanks with her after guns whilst in Boulogne harbour. On arrival in Jersey at 7.30pm, he went at once to consult with the Island's Lieutenant Governor. It was decided to provide ships and any other craft to assist in the evacuation by sea of the thousands of soldiers patiently waiting to be 'rescued' while keeping an eye open for the approach of the German Army.

The Island's potato crop was just being harvested and the usual small coasters had been engaged to load the thousands of plywood barrels of Jersey Royals and trays of tomatoes too for the English market. After his conference with the Lieutenant Governor, Commander Howard-Johnston hurried to the harbour by car and with the assistance of the harbourmaster boarded seven coasters, the 'Alt', 'Seaville', 'Hodder', 'Ouse', 'Fairfield', 'Coral' and 'Perelle' and gave their captains orders to proceed immediately to St Malo. There they were to take on board troops until they were fully loaded and then proceed to south coast ports such as Weymouth.

There was another important factor however, it was all very well to send the ships down to St Malo, but with the huge rise and fall of tide in the area, would they be able to enter the port and if they did would they get out again in reasonable time? The port had new lock gates completed in 1938 and once the tide fell too low, nothing could move through them in either direction, neither into the inner Bassin Vauban nor out again. The evacuation fleet might well have to anchor off the port and to load the soldiers from small craft.

Proving his ability once again, Commander Howard-Johnston called on the then Commodore of St Helier Yacht Club, Mr W S Le Masurier and requested that he summon all skippers of yachts and motorboats to an immediate meeting in the clubhouse. Could they provide their boats and take them to St Malo to act as tenders? There was no hesitation, everyone who could get his boat ready hurried off to do so, while others volunteered to act as crew. It was no easy task and every case was different. You see, nearly all the craft had been laid-up for the duration of the war and some had rigging, masts and equipment removed, while yet others had had the engines removed too.

Commander Howard-Johnston sailed for St Malo aboard the 'Wild Swan' that same night at 11.30pm only half-an-hour behind the first 'little ships' led by the Commodore's former RNLI lifeboat. They were 'Klang II', 'Teazer', 'Clutha' the small 'St Clement' and the States launch 'The Duchess of Normandy'. They had become ready for sea after only a few hours notice between the arrival in the Island of Commander Howard-Johnston and their departure that night for St Malo.

All night on that Sunday, 16th June, willing hands lifted and hauled and coupled up gearboxes to propeller shafts, there was so much to be done. One or two brave souls attempted to dig a channel through the harbour mud to a yacht which, high and dry, would not float on the next tide but ultimately to no avail. The hard work on these fine old wooden craft continued without a break until at last they were ready on Monday morning, within hours of their help having been requested and gladly offered.

Commander Howard-Johnston's demolition party was ready and determined to destroy the lock gates at St Malo among other vital equipment. These gates had made it possible for ships to enter the inner harbour and to remain afloat whatever the state of the tide outside the harbour. This was a valuable asset; too valuable to fall into the hands of the Kriegsmarine, who would have used it to its full potential for the maintenance and supply of quite sizeable units of their Atlantic fleet.

Another, much bigger drydock at St Nazaire was later in the war to cost the lives of many of our sailors and commandos when it was destroyed to deny the pocket battleship The 'Tirpitz' its facilities. Was it possible to destroy these gates with a small force before the arrival of the rapidly advancing enemy?

The Little Dunkirk

The good Commander decided that there was no time to spare and had sailed at 11.30pm arriving in St Malo at just before 1am on Monday. The first few yachts were quickly passed by the speeding destroyer and the others had received orders to follow as soon as possible in a separate and slower group.
They were;

'Ma Mie'	'Le Noroit'	'Sibelle'
'Fiona'	'Daddy'	'Solace'
'Desiree'	'Girl Joyce'	'Diana'
'Callou'	'Laurie'	'Lindolet'
'Peirson'		

RFC 113 47.5'
MA MIE 43'
CALLOU 41'
KLANG II 40'
EX L/BOAT 35'
CLUTHA 33'
GIRL JOYCE 32'
LE NOROIT 32'
TEAZER 32'

LINDOLET 31'
DUCHESS OF NORMANDY 30'
PEIRSON 30'
FIONA 30'
SIBELLE 30'
SOLACE 30'
DESIREE 26'
DIANA 22'
LAURIE 21'
DADDY 15'
ST. CLEMENT 15'

ST. MALO
Illustration by Frances Harris

TO JERSEY

Ref:C.1804

Some of the Jersey Yachtsmen

St Malo 1940

Ref:F.4663

SLIPWAY   BASSIN VAUBAN

LOCK GATE

Ref:F.4665

Ref:F.4658

Troops waiting to board.

Photographs courtesy of The Imperial War Museum, London

Ref:F.4671

In addition the fast motor cruiser RFC 113 which had been requisitioned and stationed in Jersey for air-sea rescue duties joined the 'fleet'.

On arrival at St Malo dock the 'Wild Swan' disembarked the demolition party in haste and immediately left the area for fear of air attack. The party split up into two groups. One group to enter the area of the oil storage tanks a little way out of St Malo while the other assessed the task of blowing up the lock gates, but not before the thousands of British and French soldiers had been taken off by the 'potato' boats and other ships. Fortunately on their arrival, the tide was high and they entered the inner 'Bassin' and berthing against the harbour walls, loaded the troops and such equipment as they had with them directly aboard. Never was a soldier better pleased to find such a smooth and timely arrival of transport. All this after the vagaries of the time wasting at Rennes racecourse, the awful descent upon St Malo on roads choked with fleeing French families among others and his less than cheerful 'welcome' in the streets of the old port itself.

As soon as loaded, the coasters made their way out of the inner harbour and set off for England. But were the efforts of the 'Jersey Fleet' then wasted and unnecessary? Not at all. Certain ships had to anchor off in the roads and the Jersey flotilla played an important role in ferrying personnel out to them. With charges secured to the gate pintles and other vital equipment set and ready to fire, it was essential that the demolition party should be taken off and furthermore, stragglers were still coming into the dock area desperately looking for any transport to England.

The Little Dunkirk

One coaster, the 'Hodder' arriving late, dropped anchor in the 'roads' outside the harbour and took aboard servicemen ferried out to her by the small boats which were loading from the ramp beneath the harbour walls normally used by the 'vedettes' which plied their trade between Dinard and St Malo. They were kept busy. Thick black smoke from the burning oil tanks hung low over the scene and the smell from the burning fuel permeated everywhere. Although the sun was shining brightly a dark shadow was cast over the dock area which contrasted with the bright light catching the buildings and coastal scenery further away. Even aboard the small boats and waiting ships the odour of men who had been unable to attend to their personal hygiene for many days formed its own backcloth to the scene and mixed with the smoke and smell of the soldiers eternal Woodbines. There was no panic, just the steady loading of a human cargo with the occasional muttered word or shout. Everyone knew of the grave danger they were in.

A French friend M Bertrand an airline 'Commandant' and author, asked me if I knew why the Luftwaffe had bombed St Helier and St Peter Port. "Because that's what they do," I replied. But he told me that the German reconnaissance aircraft overflying Brittany had spotted the small ships and activity at St Malo and had concluded that all the troops were going to both Jersey and Guernsey to reinforce the garrisons there. When they saw all the small lorries waiting patiently on the docks of both Islands they had their opinion confirmed, thinking that they were military vehicles.

Just to digress for a moment; a young Canadian Navy Lieutenant had hitch-hiked and walked from Paris where he had been attached to his embassy and came on the scene just an hour

Lee Ho

or so before the lock gates were to be blown. He chummed up with a British officer who was in the same situation and their eyes fell upon a large British Army Humber staff car. It had been abandoned at the quayside and seemed to offer the opportunity for a bit of dash and adventure. They climbed into the front seats and set off in some style to seek out the enemy's present position.

Rolling through the roads leading out to the suburbs of St Malo, they became aware of the glint of sunlight on steel among the buildings ahead of them; it was the forward scouts of the German advancing force. The big car was wrestled round in double quick time and driven at speed back to the docks to warn off the British demolition team. With a few minutes to spare before the waiting little boats embarked them, the pair realized that the Germans would soon have possession of 'their' Humber. They quickly returned to it and starting it up put it into gear and jumped clear to watch it plunge into the water of the lock.

They were ordered to board the yachts waiting for them and with one eye on the possible sudden arrival of the enemy, now close by, they were soon out in the small roads making for the open sea and Jersey. Each small boat held a mixed crew of Jerseymen, weary soldiers and other service personnel and there was also a small party of escaping civilians. The demolition of the lock gates had been a success and that huge black cloud of smoke from the fuel dump blackened the sky, obscuring the sun and towering above them in the most dramatic column. Could anything else have been supplied to heighten the tension of the moment? Just imagine the scene from sea level as these small craft with a 'bone between their teeth' ploughed out of St Malo with such a background and the certainty in the crews minds that they would be attacked from both air and from the nearby shore, but God was with them and no attacks took place.

Anxious eyes scanned the sky for the approach of enemy aircraft, the fear of being exposed to air attack while so vulnerable in small wooden boats was uppermost in their minds. Years later, one of that valiant body of men, Reg Nicolle, describing the scene to me in measured rolling tones, so typical of the man, injected a little poetic licence into his memories of the evacuation from St.Malo. "The Messerschmitts came in low across the sea and opened fire on us and swept over us with a tremendous roar. We all crouched low for fear of being hit by a bullet." When Reg had moved on, Bill Coombs who had also been aboard the small boats, walked over to me and said, "Has he been telling you about the Messerschmitts? A load of rubbish, we never even saw one!" Whatever may have been, the possibility was that the Germans would have had aircraft patrolling ahead of their ground forces and had one or two just spotted the small fleet....Elsewhere along the Breton coast accounts exist of just such attacks on small boats.

To return to our young Canadian. The individual motorboats and yachts returned to Jersey in their own time making their best possible speed. The weather was against them producing a force 4 to 5 wind 'on the nose' as sailors say, meaning that it came out of the north east kicking up a choppy sea and the worst point of sailing for the gaff-rigged yachts. Engines overheated and broke down and tows were offered and accepted, some boats were dreadfully slow so that he recalled it had taken forty-eight hours to reach Jersey, however it may just have felt like such a long period, as the sailing distance from St Malo is some thirty-two miles. They would have had to proceed at a very slow speed against strong currents and adverse winds to be quite so slow, but perhaps that was what they had to do as they had no opportunity of choosing their departure time to make best use of the tidal and weather conditions

On arrival within the pierheads at St Helier, he was put alongside a set of granite stairs leading up to the Albert Quay and there said his grateful thanks and took his leave of the Jersey crew. A long walk down the pier finished his journey from Paris which began what seemed like months ago and now he stood hungry and dishevelled outside the Pomme d'Or Hotel quite near the harbour. He entered the pleasant interior of a typical English seaside hotel and found a waiter resplendent in black bow-tie and dinner jacket, coming towards him from a nearby dining-room. "Excuse me. Would it be possible to have something to eat?" He imagined perhaps some bread and a little meat after his experience of many days spent in war torn France. "Of course, Sir. Please come this way." He was led into the dining-room and seated at a table on which white linen set off the gleaming cutlery and condiments. "Would you like the full breakfast?" It seemed like a dream. He could not know that in just a few days time a unit of the German Kriegsmarine would occupy the hotel and that they would set up German Naval Headquarters there.

The Canadian Officer returned to England safely possibly aboard the 'Rye', another coaster which was deployed to restore the demolition party and others to their distant shores. He introduced himself to me on the occasion of the unveiling of a plaque at St Helier Yacht Club in 1980 and recounted his story. At this time he was a director of Canada Dry based in London.

Boats came into the safety of St Helier Harbour after varying adventures and difficulties. Old tired engines, hastily prepared, had overheated and stopped and yachts offering a tow had had their speed reduced to a crawl. How unfamiliar the journey up to Jersey must have been for those who had found themselves aboard these small craft loaded down with various ranks and services and intermixed with civilians. How strange to those who owned or crewed the yachts as they remembered better times and took in their present 'cargo' of anxious men and women. Out of place among the winches, anchors and gear of those who often went to sea, was the glint of Lee-Enfield rifles, hand grenades, steel helmets and webbing equipment. Heavy boots and studded soles excited no comment from skippers who once would have insisted on plimsoles or bare feet on their manicured decks.

There is no record of the mooring up of the little fleet against the high granite walls of St Helier Harbour or of the many warm handshakes and muttered thanks between the crews and their guests, but I know my Jersey yachtsmen well enough to say without chance of contradiction that a quiet laugh and an embarrassed acceptance of some token of gratitude and a warm parting greeting for good luck would have been the natural order of the day. The owner of 'Clutha', W Glendewar, had the strange experience of finding an armed guard watching over his yacht when he returned to it with his crew the following day. Upon enquiring as to why he could not come aboard his own yacht he was advised that the army paymaster was below and so was the army pay chest, yet to be unloaded, hence the armed guard!

The heroic little fleet was laid-up once again and their owners saw little more of them until May 1945, some had disappeared in the hands of the German Occupying Force and were never found, others needed much work to bring them back into commission. The day came when once again St Aubin's Bay saw the return of sailing craft and motorboats.

One Jersey yacht was lying against the harbour wall in Carteret on the nearby Normandy coast, when an English gentleman on holiday looked down onto the deck from the quayside and seeing the yacht's owner, asked if the burgee fluttering at the masthead was that of St Helier Yacht Club. On hearing from the owner, Pat Gruchy, that it was, he entered into a conversation about the 'adventure' at St Malo in 1940 and introduced himself as the now Captain Howard-Johnston. After a lengthy chat, he asked whether the club had ever received any commendation or award from the Admiralty for their good work at the evacuation from St Malo. When Pat told him that they had not, he advised him to ask the club's Commodore to take this matter up with the Admiralty and that he would do what he could from the other end.

The upshot was that in May 1952 St Helier Yacht Club was granted the privilege to fly the Red Ensign defaced with the

Royal Navy emblem of an anchor combined with the crossed axes of the coat of arms of St Helier. The right to fly this 'Battle Honour' is carefully administered by the club to this day and only members holding a warrant issued by the club may fly this Ensign while they are aboard their yacht. Whenever I see this defaced ensign flying bravely in the breeze, my memory returns to those exciting days and those gallant little ships and their crews. They are indeed the spirit of St Helier Yacht Club.

I am indebted to various sources for much of the information gathered to write this chapter, but to none more so than the excellent account written by Kevin Le Scelleur in his 'Evacuation of St Malo' produced to commemorate the sixtieth anniversary of this event.

FALCONS GALORE

Was there ever before or since a class of small yacht which did more for sailing in the Channel Islands than the Falcon? Hardly a yacht, more of a dinghy, but at sixteen feet in length and heavily built of clinker construction, the Falcon was very characterful. When I first discovered them I was told that they were originally designed around a deckboat carried aboard sailing vessels hailing from the West Country and used for various purposes where a handy and seaworthy sailing boat was required.

They became a class racing dinghy around Weymouth and the south Dorset coast and found their way to the Channel Islands in the 1930's. Two 'types' soon developed, the slightly heavier Weymouth built Falcon and the lighter, more elegant Guernsey built boat. Both were virtually identical with a lovely sheer to their hulls, an identical dropkeel or centreplate and a transom mounted, substantial rudder. This could be unshipped from its pintles in a moment as with centreplate up the Falcon sailed through the shallows at the tides edge and slid up onto the sand.

The names of birds were often chosen for each delightful dinghy and so we had Cygnet, Curlew, Redshank, Shearwater, Mallard, Guillemot, Superb, Skua, Secret and so on. If the names were pleasant then even more so was the way in which each boat was tricked out by her proud owner. The hardwood rudders, thwarts centreplate boxes and every other exposed hardwood part was resplendent in carefully applied varnish as was the solid wooden, pine mast. The finely ribbed interior was usually painted in a light colour, perhaps an eggshell blue or apple green, but the hull itself was painted to perfection, each owner selecting his own colour. Even black was used, but blues and reds, greens and yellows appeared in every hue set off with often a white waterline and a carefully chosen colour below.

At the start of a major Falcon race the sea would be alive with the reflected colours of these gay little yachts as they danced up and down positioning themselves and judging the start. Starting guns fired and white smoke from them drifted across the water. The colours heightened the excitement of the moment and many people came to line the seawalls just to witness this colourful event. There was also the rush of little hulls through the water and the ruffle of transoms and rudders thrusting aside the sea as the Falcons pivoted as they 'came about' with cries from the helmsman to his two crew members of 'ready about,' 'lee ho' and sometimes 'water!' as another impeded the way of a fast moving little hull. The sight compared well with many a similar scene occurring in nature, such as a flock of seabirds alighting on the water or taking to the air.

The smell of varnish recently applied, of lightly tarred rope, hemp and cotton sails and so many other indescribable perfumes permeated each little boat. And I recall how many pretty girls laughed and moved with feline grace (though sometimes wearing oilskins) across the centreplate box. And was that just a touch of perfume in the air as I sat to leeward of that agile and determined crew member. What fun, what days!

With the starting gun fired and maybe a second gun to recall some errant boat, too keen to be away and over the line before the start, the Falcons were now in close company eyeing each other and checking every slightest move, crews adjusting their position to assist the slightest increase in boatspeed. A dab of saltspray would flick up over the weather bow and land against the breakwater on the little foredeck ahead of the mast . Slowly the little fleet spread out with sudden flurries as one would come about onto the other tack to gain an advantage or even to impede another boat. Tacking duels were often fought out within sight of a mark of the course, usually a navigational mark or large iron buoy around which the sea swirled. The buoy or mark was girt with seaweed and streaked with rust and the current of the tide carried away from it the foam or debris of the sea as the boats neared it, giving a clear warning of how it should be approached to those able to read the warning signs.

Pressed on by the fresh breeze or drifting in a gentle breath of wind, the little fleet would cut and thrust at the closest of close quarters risking minor collisions as they jockeyed for the quickest and most daring turn around the mark. Should two hulls touch there was an immediate shout of protest and some small rag of a pennant would be tied into the rigging to indicate that a protest would be placed before the Sailing Committee to be deliberated upon when the race was over. Such was the thrill and excitement of the Falcon dinghy in which so many owners and helmsmen of larger yachts often honed their skills.

As ever, Francis surprised me one day by taking me down to South Pier in St Helier Harbour and showing me his new possession, 'Redshank,' a lovely Weymouth built Falcon. She sat there in her cradle on the beach among the other Falcons glowing red and showing her gleaming varnish work. That was the beginning of many fondly remembered days 'at sea'. We nursed her and coaxed her, varnished her and polished her and enjoyed every minute of it. What a delight those little craft were. 'Swallows and Amazons', they had all the spirit of that delightful book.

We never did particularly well in racing with Redshank, we had too much to learn, but that did not matter to us in the slightest. Perhaps our best race together was a long distance one. It was to Guernsey and was an 'open' event in which we could compete. The early morning start saw a grey sky and more than enough wind, but we set off with a small fleet of various yachts and although pressing on at five knots with a good breeze we were soon 'tail-end-Charlie'. The sea was as the French weather boys say, "un peu agite." In other words, decidedly not for Falcons or any other small open yachts.

We rose and fell and twisted and squirmed for more than six long hours. Our sole comfort was a small primus stove suspended from the boom to boil water to make tea! At last we arrived in Guernsey to find that under handicap we had done quite well. A Guernsey friend, David Feak met us and as we stood on 'terra firma' the ground rose and swayed beneath our feet. We hurried to David's nearby house and fell asleep immediately.

The characters who owned, helmed or crewed the Falcons was a study in itself. Bob Kempster was the first who comes to mind. A grower or small farmer from the coastal area at La Rocque, Bob had been brought up in small rowing and sailing boats since his earliest days. Many farming families kept a small boat to use for fishing to supplement the food on the table and their income too. But it was the La Rocque Regatta which caught the attention and imagination of the young Bob. This was the annual event which brought out every form of small sailing and rowing boat to compete in a variety of races. The 'rules of engagement' were few and far between, in fact I believe that none existed in writing, so that deliberate collisions were the norm and the heavy little La Rocque fishing boats could deliver a hefty clout.

On one celebrated occasion, so Bob told me, one small boat rammed another in the side so hard that the planks were cracked and broken. She began to take in water and to sink, but the owner threw her quickly onto the opposite tack to bring the damaged area out of the water, tore off his oilskins and quickly producing a hammer and tacks nailed his oilskins across the broken planks and sailed on to win! Yet again when a sea mist had descended on the racing fleet, which was more or less becalmed, the Committee boat, which observed all the 'infringements' of the 'Rules', hailed into view. The gentlemen of the Committee called out to the small La Rocque fishing boat which lay still upon the sea, "Have you seen the -------", a well-known rock and mark of the course. "Seen it!" yelled back the worthy skipper of the LRFB, "I'm Bl**dy sitting on it!"

During the German Occupation some fishing boats were permitted by our German 'guests' to sail out of La Rocque to ply their trade. Always with an armed soldier aboard to prevent escape to the nearby French coast or even to England. Bob recounted the times when the proud member of the Wehrmacht was too sick to prevent anything yet Bob could not leave for fear of repercussions on his family.

'Guillemot' was Bob's Falcon. Pale blue and perhaps not the best kept of the fleet, in Bob's hands she outsailed every other

Falcons Galore

Falcon. Was it the boat? No, it was Bob's natural instinct for the sea and its every whim. Bob could sit there at the helm nonchalantly discussing the weather, the potato crop or whatever, yet nursing his little craft out in front of the pursuing fleet. He was a pleasure to be with. His weatherbeaten yet young looking face frequently creased with pleasure and his blue eyes twinkled as he laughed out loud with his signature staccato laugh.

Many happy moments with Bob spring to mind. Once when I was Secretary of the Falcons, I was approached and asked to have 'Guillemot' measured. A group of owners were concerned that Bob's and 'Guillemots' unbroken run of successes could not be explained and thought that the strict class rules must have been broken. Looking round for an impartial judge I struck upon another character, Ronnie Taylor, sometimes known as 'Rocky'. Ronnie was then the assistant Harbourmaster and knowledgeable about matters to do with the sea and boats. He owned a lovely Solent one-design class yacht, 'Swallow'.

Accepted by one and all as their 'judge' and 'measurer' Ronnie repaired with me by arrangement to Bob's barn. The lair of the 'Guillemot'. There lay the 'Guillemot' or should I say, hung the 'Guillemot' for Bob had her suspended by the forestay chainplate on the bow and her rudder fastenings so that her hull just caressed the earthen floor of the barn. Bob murmured something to us about inducing a banana shape to the hull and we began to measure according to all the laid down figures. We even weighed and checked the heavy drop keel, an iron plate of over a hundred pounds weight. Nothing was outside the limits. All was well with the 'Guillemot'.

Why were other owners so concerned? Let me give you a little illustration. Every year a Falcon Regatta was held against our friends of the Weymouth Club. Their team came on alternate years to Jersey while we sent our team in like manner to Weymouth on the other years. It was good fun and our chosen helmsmen accommodated their opponents. The whole Regatta was topped off with the Falcon Dinner, quite a little event in itself. Eight Falcons were supplied by the local owners and the boats were drawn by lot, four to the Jersey team and four to the visiting team. In the morning race the visitors sailed their four yachts against the local team and in the afternoon, the teams changed over Falcons and sailed the same course. The combined scores produced the final score and proclaimed the winning team.

On the particular year in question Bob won the morning race in his allocated boat and in the afternoon race he was given the Falcon which had been last boat home in the morning race. He won again with that Falcon too.

However, a certain amount of resentment was circulating among a few of the class owners and a little and quite unimportant plot was being hatched to deprive Bob of a race should he win it. I got wind of this and felt it was mean and unworthy of this sporting group. You must understand that the Falcon, being little more than a dinghy, was not equipped for longer coastal passages and carried no flares, compass, water or other navigational or safety equipment. Certain fixtures of St Helier Yacht Club's racing calendar were fairly long distance events, such as the 'Round the Island' race and they were open to all classes of yacht competing under handicap.

Part of the rules applicable to the races required that all competing craft should carry full safety equipment and certain navigational aids.

The scheme to undo Bob, our gentle farmer, was that at the end of the race someone would ask to see his equipment. On the morning of the race, before leaving home I took a small sailbag and placed in it all the 'required' equipment and took it onto my yacht. Well before the start of the race, while many yachts were coming to the area of the start line, I sailed alongside Guillemot and asked Bob had he any of the items needed. "What?", he yelled, "Oh, I haven't bothered with all that rubbish!" I passed over the little canvas bag and asked Bob to put it up in the bow under the cuddy and out of the way of spray and told him that if he was asked to show his equipment to open and display its contents.

The weight of a small bag presented no problem to Bob and off he sailed. At the end of the race, in which Bob had placed, I was nearby alongside the Victoria Pier tied up with other yachts awaiting the tide to get onto our moorings, when two heads and shoulders appeared on the quay high above us and a voice called down, "Bob." Bob looked up. "Bob. Can you show us your compass please." "Oh, all right," said the owner of 'Guillemot' and going forward, produced the sailbag and undoing its cord fumbled around inside and produced a neat little handbearing compass he had never seen before. He held it up for inspection from on high. There was a stunned silence from the 'inspectors'. After a moment, "Is that OK," asked Bob. "Oh, yes," stammered down a voice to us, "Can we see your water please?" Again a fumbling and the production of a bottle of the required liquid. "Thank you," and discomfited, they disappeared from view. Bob grinned from ear to ear and passed the sailbag to me.

Ah, you will think, this was a little unfair. After all he should have met the rules, but look at it this way. Bob was a gifted helmsman, a 'natural', knowing little or nothing of racing rules and measurements. We used to smile and say that you could put Bob in a bathtub and given an oar with which to steer it and a sail, he would win a race. Had the 'inspectors' really entered into the spirit of sailing they should have had a quiet word with Bob before the race started.

Bob went onto bigger things and was asked to helm large yachts which he did successfully. It was unfortunate that during an offshore night race off the Minquiers he received a head injury when struck by the yacht's boom. Although he fully recovered from this, I always felt that Bob was affected by that incident. I pay tribute to a wonderful Jerseyman and a good friend.

John Thuiller was an entirely different man. A banker employed by the St Helier branch of Lloyd's Bank he was intelligent and studied tactics in racing. John was of Irish descent and spoke with the clipped accents of a Dublin man. His Falcon, 'Cygnet', had a varnished hull and was kept to perfection. Johnnie Thuillier was always chosen for our team events and had a host of silver trophies on his sideboard. You were doing very well in a race if you kept up with 'Cygnet'.

It was, I suppose, the introduction of plastics into yachting that saw the demise of the Falcon and in a small way, I was inevitably caught up in this. As secretary of the Falcons, I had heard good reports of the latest sailing development, terylene sails. Now, by the rules, all Falcon sails had to be cotton and made to a particular pattern and dimensions. So it was not unexpected that when I suggested at a Falcon Committee Meeting that the members should consider adopting this new material, that it should be considered, but rejected.

I now owned 'Redshank', having bought her for £125 from Francis, who had bought the beautiful Dragon class yacht, 'Lalun'. Not abashed, I decided to order a suit of terylene sails for my own pleasure and made this known to several members including Johnnie. "Remember, you will not be allowed to race with them", he said.

When the sails arrived I was surprised how stiff and white they were, so unlike their cotton counterparts. I had a job to fit the mainsail to the boom, but at last, with Yvonne aboard, my lovely staff nurse and ex St Helier Yacht Club Cadet, we sailed out on a lovely spring morning and and began to break in the new sails along the waters edge inside St Aubin's Bay.

After an hour or two we spotted 'Cygnet' well astern of us as we headed back towards the harbour. Just for amusement, I shipped a small Seagull outboard motor I happened to be carrying aboard and started it up. We were too far away for Johnnie to see what was going on. With the engine ticking over and our new sails set we soon opened up a nice lead on 'Cygnet'.

As soon as we reached our mooring, I removed the motor and stowed it away in the bow cuddy. 'Cygnet' entered her cradle gently, not too far away from us among the resting Falcons. "Those new terylene sails work well," said 'Cygnets' owner. "You certainly left me behind." I had no difficulty in having terylene sails accepted under the rules at the next Falcon meeting and they were much better than the cotton ones. But it was the 'swansong' of the Falcon, to mix a species.

But there were other moments too....One summer evening Yvonne and I sailed out of the harbour together just to enjoy 'Redshank', the St Aubin's Bay and the setting sun and, of course most young men will know what it is like to be alone with a pretty girl! We 'cruised' around the bay often close to the waters edge and the sun set as a light zephyr of a breeze made the bow chuckle through the calm sea. We noticed the welcoming lights of the old port of St Aubin start to glimmer and we specially noticed the lights of the 'Old Courthouse', one of our favourite drinking haunts. With some difficulty in the falling light we checked the little tidetable booklet, Yes! There was just a nice amount of tide left to allow us to paddle ashore in our shorts and to get back to 'Redshank' while she still floated. Centreplate up and rudder unshipped we caressed the beach and secured her on her anchor. It was a moments work to drop the sails and soon I was ordering two Mary Ann Specials at the bar in the cosy atmosphere of the pub.

Now tidetables are very accurate, giving the times and heights of tides to minutes and inches, but they are also set out by a page to a month. Therefore, if you read the wrong page you will be a long way out! It was the month of July and we, in the falling light had read the data for the month of June.

'Redshank' stood at an unusual angle on the dry beach, this was bad, because we could not drag her down to the receding tide, but worse still she had dried out on a large stone which had broken a bottom plank. When the tide returned she would not float, but would fill with water. I had no idea how to salvage her and it was now about ten o'clock. Bob Kempster would know what to do! We hurried to a phone box and called Bob at La Rocque. Bob did not offer advice. He immediately understood our predicament and asked me where exactly the boat lay. Then he told us to wait beside her on the beach.

Within half-an-hour or so I heard the engine of the typical little one and a half ton farmer's lorry coming across the beach and Bob arrived, all smiles and confident and glad of the challenge. "Let's get her over," he said. All three of us hauled on the mainsail halliard and the top of the mast came gradually over so that the hull tipped onto its starboard side and the damaged area of the portside of the hull was clearly accessible. Bob went to his lorry and came back with a roll of roofing felt, some thick black roofing adhesive, copper tacks and a few tools. In no time at all he had covered the damaged area with a substantial and waterproof patch. The rest was easy, and with Yvonne safely at home I returned to 'Redshank' in the early hours of the morning and sailed her back onto the moorings. Needless to add, I am always particularly careful to check the month when I refer to a tidetable!

To the best of my knowledge, as I write this, only two Falcons are still afloat and kept in fine condition by John Raffray ('Merlin' now named 'Scheherazade') and Kay Jackson ('Cygnet'). The fleet slowly dwindled as fibreglass and terylene swept into yacht construction. One can understand why. The old wooden hulls were constantly in need of maintenance and often leaked. They were becoming expensive to repair as yard prices increased and so owners slowly turned to the new materials. But not without some resistance.

I recall one night in Granville on the nearby Normandy coast when the young French Matelots 'steamed' through the restaurants where all our yachtsmen (and 'yachtswomen' too!) were resting after their labours of the race. A group would surround your table and friendly, if somewhat suffused with drink faces, would demand, "Coque en bois ou plastique, M'sieu?" and if you replied "Bois" they danced with pleasure around the table singing some song which even at that time I could not translate with my limited knowledge of French.

So it was that the lovely Falcon fleet declined and faded away, but by now I was crewing a Dragon.

IT PAYS TO TAKE CARE

Jimmy Muir was a local hotelier whose family owned the Sunshine Hotel at Havre des Pas and the Jubilee Hotel on the Esplanade in St Helier among other ventures. Both he and his good friend Eddie Worrel, a telephone engineer, were experienced motorboat sailors. Sometimes your imagination can get the better of you, and so it was with this intrepid pair.

Jimmy had acquired a twelve foot outboard motor speedboat. It was of the typical configuration for the 1960's; a wrap round windscreen and an open cockpit with two quite comfortable upholstered seats, a dashboard, steering wheel, gear and throttle lever adjacent to the 'driver' and of course a largish petrol fuelled outboard motor. It could speed around St Aubin's Bay at around 20 knots and consumed a great deal of fuel in doing so. Great fun! As long as you remembered that it was not meant for anything more than 'round the bay' work in very calm weather.

It was amusing to drive and I spent one or two enjoyable jaunts towing the deputy harbourmaster, at that time Captain Ronnie Taylor, on waterskis behind this little craft. But take it to sea, go to the French coast, perhaps St Malo, never. You can see the temptation though, can't you. Only one and a half hours to St

Malo, but, hello, Granville was even closer on the east coast of Normandy. Only one hour away.

The temptation was too much for Jimmy and he persuaded Eddie to join him on a quick daytrip to Granville, perhaps a spot of lunch and a drink or two then back home to Jersey! So….they took all the precautions, plenty of fuel in the tank and spare fuel in jerricans, charts and navigational gear, a compass etc, and on a nice sunny day they took off in the morning for a spin down to Granville.

I had driven down to St Helier Yacht Club in the middle of the afternoon for a cup of tea and a chat and was just parking my Rover 75 when I spotted two bedraggled figures streaming water from their clothes as they walked and looking rather forlorn. It looked like Jimmy and Eddie so I walked towards them and they were just recognizable. I thought that they must have fallen out of a dinghy into the harbour, but they were shivering with cold and looked more than a little shaken. My offer of a lift was readily accepted and on the way round to the hotel on the Esplanade and later over a drink they told me of their adventure.

As is so often the case, all had gone well as the little speedboat and its gallant crew departed the harbour and rounded the Demie des Pas light on its tall granite tower and set course for Granville, only a little over twenty miles away as the crow flies. Very quickly the Chausey reef and group of islets hove into sight. Things were going well. What a doddle! The wind which had been behind them now increased steadily in strength and they found themselves beginning to plane down the face of modest waves. The planing increased and became a little hectic. Some jockeying with the throttle became necessary, but after

It Pays To Take Care

several minutes it was obvious that they were no longer spinning along towards Chausey and later Granville, but were fighting to just keep their little open craft afloat. The Granville lunch was now a distant dream and as for the drink or two, what would they have given for just one at that moment!

The decision was made to turn back for St Helier only half-an-hour away, but half-an-hour at twenty knots how long at two knots? Timing their turn they shipped a little water as they manoeuvred between waves. But now they were running into waves which would have presented no problem to a capable seagoing yacht, motor or sail, but to an inshore speedboat they were too much. Even at the slowest speed seas climbed over the little varnished foredeck and assisted by the sloping windscreen slopped in substantial amounts over the crew, once comfortable in their padded seats, but now sitting deep in cold water.

It was only the skill, courage and luck which now came to their aid that saved them as their craft began to swamp. Eddie clambered into the stern and his weight there balanced the hull a little better and he began to bail out the seawater and to lift the fuel tank to a higher level in case it became contaminated and the motor stopped. Jimmy played with the throttle and eased the cockleshell speedboat over crest after crest hardly noticing the slow approach of the Demie on its high tower, so easily passed what seemed like hours before.

Now a new problem presented itself as the motor began to cough and race and splutter. FUEL! Eddie needed no further warning and grabbed a jerrican of petrol. On dry land it is never too easy to handle a heavy can of fuel and to splash its inflammable contents into a funnel resting in the fuel filler pipe of a tank, but in a rocking boat with the engine running it was a different world. Petrol poured everywhere and some went down into the tank, but most went into the hull and over the stern into the sea. The biggest problem was not to fall overboard when holding the jerrican with both hands. Eddie found himself hugging a vibrating motor which was also twisting under him as Jimmy steered the little boat which demanded a lot of steering at slow speed. At last Eddie thought that enough fuel (and some seawater too!) had got into the engine and fastened down the filler cap. In fact it did take several hours to pass the tower and turn for St Helier Harbour. They had limped in through the pierheads and tied up to their moorings, just before I had met up with them. They knew that they had nearly drowned themselves. A less experienced pair would not have survived. They never attempted a similar trip again….but others still do!

I was just untying my dinghy from the pontoon in St Aubin's Harbour in the 1990's when I noticed five men getting aboard a fibreglass 'dorey' just a short distance from me. They had some difficulty starting up the big outboard motor due to lack of experience and one or two of the crew caught my eye and laughed. They were a gang of Irish lads and their accents echoed off the sunlit high granite walls of the old harbour. Resting from their labours in trying to start their engine, they called across to me enquiring directions for Guernsey!

Well, you don't just say, "Go out through the pierheads and turn right at Noirmont Point," do you? So I asked them if they had their chart there and I would point out the course on it. "Ah sure we don't have a chart, it's just us" and they looked around among themselves and laughed. I know and understand the Irish temperament and humour well as my mother was of west of

Ireland stock, so I said, "You'll have a compass though?" The answer was in the negative and they went on to say that they had just bought the boat the previous night in a bar! A few more subtle questions, as I sat there in my dinghy, revealed that they were totally unequipped. No flares, no lifejackets, no radio, no water, nothing. I advised them that their Guernsey 'jaunt' was out of the question and that they should buy some equipment before they even went out of the pierheads. They laughed and thanked me cheerfully, giving me a fool's pardon and with the motor now running shot through the pierheads in great style. The luck of the Irish!

An entirely different affair, but with similarities as you will see. Yvonne and I were lying in St Peter Port harbour aboard 'Blue Raven' our beautiful Dutch cruising yacht. We were alongside a new French built aluminum yacht of about thirty-five feet overall. She was purposeful and well fitted out. Her owner, young and well-built with dark curly hair was attempting to climb the mast on this sunny summer day with the assistance of his 'crew'. The 'crew' was the most beautiful Caribbean girl, graceful and happy. She was trying to haul her skipper up the mast as he sat in a bosun's chair, but he weighed twelve stone and I imagine she weighed in at nine or thereabouts. He was attempting to retrieve a halliard which had been allowed to run up the mast. Yvonne and I immediately offered to help and soon had the job done.

Now standing on his deck our new French friend introduced himself and his girlfriend. They had taken delivery of their new yacht at La Rochelle the day before and were making their way to Paris. Would we join them for a drink? We gladly accepted and went below. The yacht was specially finished to her owner's requirements and was very, very different. She was wide and had comfortable settee berths around the main saloon and, centrally placed, a quite large bar enclosing a refrigerator of generous proportions. What would we like to drink, perhaps our host could suggest a Caribbean punch? His suggestion having proved acceptable, the girl squatted elegantly down in front of the bar and quickly prepared four glasses of a superb, memorable drink. It was lovely to see her graceful movements and skill.

We were then invited to see around the yacht and were shown into the forward cabin. It was huge and contained a Breton bed with the carved sliding doors of the type which is seen in a farmhouse. All to the design of the owner. The whole yacht was in much the same vein throughout and I could see that Yvonne was greatly impressed as I certainly was.

With our drinks now refreshed by our hostess we began to discuss their voyage so far. Could I point out the course through Guernsey waters? I asked for his chart and was told that he had none aboard! "But surely you must have used a chart to come up to Guernsey from La Rochelle?" "No". Apparently it was considered unnecessary. I went aboard 'Blue Raven' and brought a spare chart and showed the French skipper the passage out to the north east for which he was very grateful. We thanked them for their hospitality and they left for Paris. It makes you wonder!

Long before I became interested in sailing, it must have been in the early fifties, I recall and incident which got into the newspapers. An ex-navy or perhaps ex-army 'Fairmile', a service launch of about one hundred and twenty feet was seen on the Thames running downriver. She was badly handled and bumped into buoys and impeded other yachts on her wayward course. At last she hit a large metal fairway marker buoy and sustained some damage. Nearby was a shipyard where the owner had stood watching this floating disaster unfolding. Seeing the damaged yacht now moored to the buoy, he got into the yard launch and went over to her. He offered to tow the yacht into his yard and his offer of help was accepted. Some repairs were put in hand and the crew, a young family of four, climbed up the staircase to the office to have some tea.

"Tell me", said the 'yard owner, "where are you going with that large motorboat, because from here you will soon be at sea." The answer surprised him. The 'Fairmile' and its very inexperienced crew were off to East Africa to start a new life there! "But," said the 'yard owner, "I haven't seen a chart table or any navigational equipment aboard your boat." It transpired that their navigational equipment consisted of a child's school atlas and a twelve inch school ruler! He was further informed that you don't need more than that. Because the boat would be 'driven' down the Thames where the riverbanks will guide you and when you reach the sea you turn right and follow any ship going in your direction. But what about entering the Mediterranean, supposing you got that far? Oh that was easy too. It is the only big entry on your left and you get out at the far end easily because there is only one exit, The Suez canal!

It does not happen often? I could go on and on. A local schoolteacher bought a fine cruising yacht of twenty-nine feet an 'Elizabethan'. I was surprised for I never thought that he had any interest in the sea whatever. To cut a very lengthy story short, he entered a race to 'Binic' on the Brittany coast and had an equally 'knowledgeable' crew aboard. They were doing surprisingly well and were up with the leaders when the owner announced

It Pays To Take Care

after several hours of sailing that they were turning round and going back to Jersey. Oh yes, he had all the necessary charts, but he had reached the edge of the first one and did not know how to find his position on the next overlapping chart! No it does not happen often or does it?

It was a wintry day, cold, but dry with just a hint of sunshine when I was working on 'Faeiriedell', our twenty-seven foot Dell Quay Ranger. It was my first venture into motorboating and I was completing her restoration at St Aubin's Harbour in Jersey. The boat was raised up high on blocks ashore on the quay conveniently situated opposite to the Old Courthouse and The Royal Channel Islands Yacht Club. So I was well placed for liquid refreshment. Placed half way along the quay and right up to the edge of the land tie, the view over the port side was a dizzy fifty foot drop to the mud and moored dinghies below and continued across every part of the harbour.

It was lunchtime, but I was preoccupied with the job in hand and enjoying the task, as nearly all yachtsmen do, when I thought I might have heard a faint cry from far off. It could have been children playing, however I stopped what I was doing and cocked an ear to see if I heard it again. Perhaps it was just a seabird, seagulls can make some very human sounding noises as they 'sail' overhead. There it was again. It sounded like a distorted "Help". I scrambled into the cockpit and swept the view for any sign of trouble or distress, but there was nothing to be seen. I was alone on the quay.

Then the cry came again and I focused on the dinghies far below lying on their moorings and now afloat on the incoming tide. Could that be a head in the water between those dinghies and then I saw the hands too grasping the gunnel of a small wooden dinghy. I was out of the cockpit and down the short ladder in a moment and running to the rough granite steps which lead to the wooden pontoon floating against the harbour wall. There he was, an elderly man who I knew by sight as he was member of the nearby club.

His head was just above the water and his white hands curled over the dinghy's wooden rubbing strake. He was calling out, "Help", but weakly and the water must have been very cold. I scrambled across several little hulls and at last gripped his wrists which were icy cold. I knew that there was no chance that I could pull him over the side in such a small craft. I quickly pulled the little boat into the side of the pontoon and fastened its painter to the tierail. Then gripped both his wrists and dragged him, still in the water to the bow and somehow rolled my lower half onto the pontoon where I was now lying flat. A quick pant to get my breath back and I squatted down holding both wrists.

Now, could I lift him out? He may have weighed about fifteen stone, his clothes were soaked and he was quite unable to help me, but still conscious. I suppose he must have been in the water for some time before I arrived on the scene. Settling myself into a good position, I tried to pull him the eighteen inches or so from the water level onto the pontoon. I could hardly move him at all. By now I did not care what damage I did to his clothes if only I could get him out! I shouted for help, which was difficult as I was facing the water and could only turn my head a little to either side. I doubted whether anyone was about to hear me and I knew that I had to be quick.

It Pays To Take Care

I decided to 'moor' the man to the side of the pontoon while I went quickly for help. There was plenty of tailends of dinghy moorings scattered around on the deck of the pontoon and I quickly passed one around his back under his arms and tightly onto the tubular metal rail of the pontoon. He could not slip away, but hypothermia was the danger so I could not waste time. I clambered up the ancient and awkward granite steps and ran as quickly as I could towards the Old Courthouse for help. Just at the end of the pier, sitting on a raised step with his back to the wall, was a young artist in his twenties sketching the scene. "Quick, come with me, there's a man drowning", I spoke with determination as I knew he must come without unnecessary delay or lengthy explanation. He was quick-witted and jumped to his feet following me as I ran back to the stairs and raced down to the pontoon. I untied my rope and together with one hand gripping his collar and the other underwater under his belt on the count of three we shot him up out of the water to lie like a stranded dolphin with water streaming from his clothes.

There was no need for resuscitation as he was breathing, but gasping for breath. After some time, he had recovered enough to be helped to his feet and we managed to regain the quay where I wanted to bring an ambulance to meet us. However, he would not hear of that and instead we made our way to The Royal Channel Islands Yacht Club where he was cared for immediately. Some days later, he came along to me as I was continuing the work on my boat and thanked me and added that he had sent a donation of fifty pounds to the R.N.L.I as a token of his appreciation.

I have told this event because I know of several similar occurrences which did not have a happy ending and hope that it may serve as a warning to be so careful when on and around boats whether they are on the moorings or out at sea. If you slip off a wet or icy pontoon and fall into the mud between moored yachts or even into the water you are in great danger of not being found if you cannot help yourself perhaps because of an injury. I recall an incident on the south coast when exactly this happened at night to a yachtsman. Fortunately he had a mobile phone with him, but even then his rescuers had the greatest difficulty in finding him hidden between two yachts and camouflaged with mud.

A TRAGEDY OF MISHAPS

It was quite a sky. Yvonne and I wondered at the strange yellowish colour and even stranger still the threatening atmosphere. We had driven to St Helier Yacht Club and now stood on the open first floor balcony gazing out to sea beyond the small roads and the fine Victorian breakwater of Elizabeth Castle. High winds, very high winds indeed were forecast. You must understand that in 1964 we did not have the advantage of the sophisticated weather forecasting that yachtsmen and others enjoy today. Ours was more allied to the old sciences of the Jersey folklore and to watching the 'glass'. There was definitely a foreboding in the air and we knew that it was not the time to be at sea.

The 'Maricelia' was a large, by Jersey standards of the day, a very large, motoryacht, described in Lloyd's Register of Yachts as a twin screw schooner. She weighed in at thirty-two tons Thames Measurement and was just over fifty-six feet long and had a beam of twelve feet. Drawing five feet of water she was designed for serious motor cruising. Built in 1939 in James A Silver's 'yard at Rosneath, of a type generally referred to as 'Silver' yachts she was propelled by two Gardner four cylinder engines. Beautifully maintained by her owner Mr James M

Fraser, 'Maricelia' was registered in Jersey as her home port although the family lived in England.

'Maricelia' had set out from Jersey well before any announcement of impending bad weather had been mooted about and arrived safely in St Malo for a short holiday with the family aboard. St Malo has always been a Mecca for the more proficient yachtsman and has much to offer in the grandeur of its old walled town, quaint streets and truly Malouine atmosphere. While enjoying the wonderful fresh seafood in one of the many restaurants, yachtsmen were often captivated by troubadours wandering the narrow streets and performing song, mime or dance for the sheer pleasure of it.

So it was with the 'crew' of the Maricelia, but misfortune visited them in the shape of an accident aboard which left Mrs Fraser with a broken arm. This must have caused much pain to the family not to mention disruption to their plans. The minor fire which broke out on another day was quickly overcome, but coming on top of the accident to Mrs Fraser it convinced 'Maricelia's' owner that he should head home immediately so that his wife could be in the care of her own doctor and in the comfort of her home to rest and to get well. At the same time the yacht could be repaired by the Southpier Shipyard where she was well known.

But you will recall the impending storm already mentioned with its yellowing sky and foreboding atmosphere. I can well understand how Mr Fraser felt. He probably had little warning of the weather in store for him if he left St Malo, cocooned as he was inside the inner basin, the Bassin Vauban and sheltering under the high ramparts of the old town. His wife needed her home, the yacht was large and capable and he was well crewed. They could leave St Malo and be in St Helier only thirty-two miles away in three hours. They sailed.

As we islanders often do at the height of a strong gale, when the hurricane force winds were at their most furious, Bill Morvan drove his car along the country roads full of leaves stripped from the trees and small branches too. He had just left his work at the Telecommunications Department at Jersey Airport and instead of going home headed for Noirmont Point a promontory overlooking the approaches to St Helier and with an extensive view to the Minquiers and on a clear day beyond that to the cliffs of Cap Frehel with its twin lighthouse towers on the north Brittany coast thirty-two miles distant.

The winds shrieked in from the south west at Force twelve and the sea was shrouded by spume and spray torn from the waves. It was an awe inspiring sight. The visibility was not good and the violence of the wind rocked the car and outside made it difficult to breathe let alone stand still. Bill was no ordinary spectator, he was a skilled yachtsman of many years experience soon to be the Commodore of St Helier Yacht Club and later a Senator of the States of Jersey and President of the Harbours and Airport Committee.

He gazed out over the dramatic seascape and no doubt thought what it would be like to be caught out in that weather in a small yacht. But, what was that! A hull broke through the seas and crashed on through wave after wave driving to the east in the direction of St Helier. Bill struggled to open the car door and reached into the glove compartment where he kept his binoculars. Then the awful realization; the yacht was out of control. Focusing as best he could in the conditions, Bill saw that, although running at speed, she had no wheelhouse or any vestige of superstructure left above her teak laid decks and worse still, he could see from his vantage point that there was no one at the wheel! There was only a dark void reaching down into the interior of the hull. A strange vivid light flashed occasionally deep down in the interior as though to add more drama to the awful sight. Perhaps the large bank of batteries had broken loose, Bill thought. What disaster had overcome this yacht? Not waiting a minute longer, he forced his way back into the car and drove at speed to the nearest phone to call out the lifeboat.

The 'Elizabeth Rippon' was the Royal National Lifeboat Institution's lifeboat stationed afloat on a mooring close to the crew's quarters on the Albert Quay. As soon as the maroons went up and resounded, echoing across the harbour and the town of St Helier, a crew dropped everything and descended at maximum speed on the Quay. In no time moorings were cast off and the coxswain Ted Larbalestier headed his craft for the pierheads to face whatever lay waiting for them in this full hurricane with winds gusting in excess of one hundred and fifty miles an hour.

Gordon Coombs, whose family owned Southpier Shipyard, was a highly respected skipper of some of the bigger motoryachts moored in St Helier Harbour and was also a lifeboatman. Crewmen always consider themselves lucky if they make it on time to the 'launch' of the lifeboat, for the coxswain cannot wait, but leaves as soon as he feels that he has a crew aboard. The crew all know of the difficulties with traffic and other delays, but the boat must launch on time. They pride themselves on the speed of the launch from the first warning to dropping the moorings. Gordon made it this time.

A Tragedy Of Mishaps

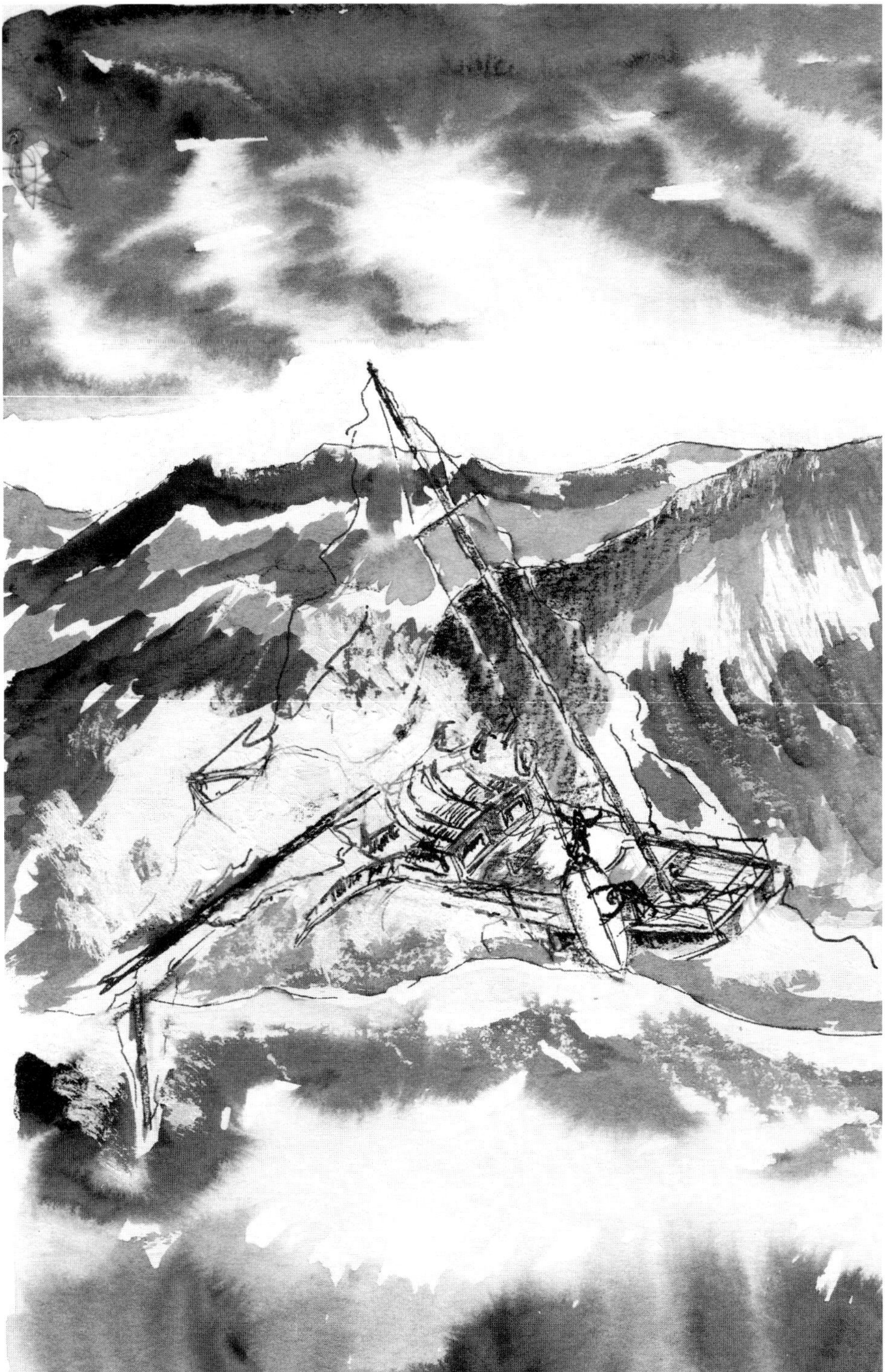

On the deck of the lifeboat it was difficult to speak against the force of the wind. Voices were torn away by the gale and the little boat tossed and heeled as she cleared the high harbour walls and set off down the 'small' roads. So often on a fine summer day many skippers had jilled along this passage and gazed around at the fortifications of Elizabeth Castle and the granite reefs which lay ahead. This was a very very different day. The sight which met their eyes was one of a torn sea and hurtling spray which flew horizontally into their faces making it almost impossible to see. Even the colours of the sea and sky were far removed from normal.

The coxswain fought the wheel and forced his strong craft towards the Platte Beacon, the red painted metal lattice tower and outer marker warning shipping away from the Castle breakwater and outlying rocks. But before they had even reached it, a large white hull came crashing through the seas across their line of vision and on a steady heading plunged rolling heavily and tossing her bow towards Grève d'azette narrowly missing the East Rock and the Dog's Nest. Their impression as the hull crossed their course, was of a huge yacht wrecked by the sea in a most terrible way. Surely great seas had swept across her from bow to stern to tear her strong teak superstructure out by the roots. As she rolled and travelled on her doomed way, they could see down into the interior and search her below decks cabin layout for any sign of life aboard, but on her, not a soul was to be seen.

The coxswain swung his wheel to port knowing that, there was not the slightest chance of catching up with the wreck and very little chance of boarding her if they did. The crew all watched the 'Maricelia', for indeed it was her, tear through the reef and come to a calamitous, shuddering end on the reef off the beach at Grève d'azette. What had happened to her, what violent event had torn apart a well-found yacht of the best construction?

We will never know exactly where or when or what decisions were made which brought about this disaster, but it is believed that the yacht was making her passage up to Jersey by the west of the Minquiers and was hoping to catch the tide as it turned towards Jersey. As the weather worsened, enormous waves rolled down on the 'Maricelia' making steering enormously difficult when, suddenly, a wave even greater than the others, climbed hideously across the large open foredeck and crashed through the wheelhouse windows. Mr Fraser was seriously injured about the face and must have reacted quickly putting the yacht into selfsteering mode while he grappled with his injuries and the wrecked condition of his wheelhouse.

Some of the family saw that the yacht's motorboat, referred to as a 'shark boat', had broken loose and, not realizing the danger they were putting themselves into, went on deck to secure it. Another great wave must have swept them away and the shark boat with them. Was it the same powerful wave which destroyed the wheelhouse and afterdeck superstructure? We cannot know, but no one was found aboard the hull so that we can assume that Mr and Mrs Fraser were also tragically lost at about this time. The crewless hulk now continued, still under selfsteering gear, with both Gardner engines running on its final course towards St Helier and its violent end.

You would think that no one could survive such a calamity, but one young girl did Alison Mitchell was a friend of the family and had been invited for the cruise down to St Malo. Now,

A Tragedy Of Mishaps

terrified out of her mind, caught in the vicelike grip of nature at its wildest, she found herself in a violent sea with little or no chance of rescue. A strong swimmer, she saw the shark boat, upturned and awash, her only chance of survival. Struggling with the wet and pitching hull she managed to drag herself across the centre of the hull and hung on to the keel for dear life.

Washed by seas, as night fell, she would realize that the strong rising tide was carrying her around the island of Jersey in an anti-clockwise direction. At times from the crest of a wave she could see the coastline so far away and clung on to the insecure perch. She may have fallen asleep or become unconscious, but after an interminable period of time she knew that she was near the shore and the high cliffs on the north coast of Jersey. She slipped into the water, exhausted and more dead than alive, swam towards the rocks and then started the long and difficult climb.

A farmer in his yard was attending to his morning chores when he was startled to see the most dreadful apparition coming towards him, frightening him greatly it was Alison She had scaled the cliffs, struggled through gorse, brambles and the undergrowth and now staggered towards him with arms outstretched, groaning a plea for help. After hours immersed in the sea and following her courageous struggle over the rocks and up the cliffs, scratched and bloodied and with dishevelled hair, her skin bloated by the saltwater, she presented a terrible sight. He regained his senses and she was soon tended to in the farmhouse and an ambulance was called. It took days for her to recover.

I was present at the yacht club when her father came to thank us all for searching for the crew. He had the haunted appearance of a man who had looked into the abyss and by some chance had come back.

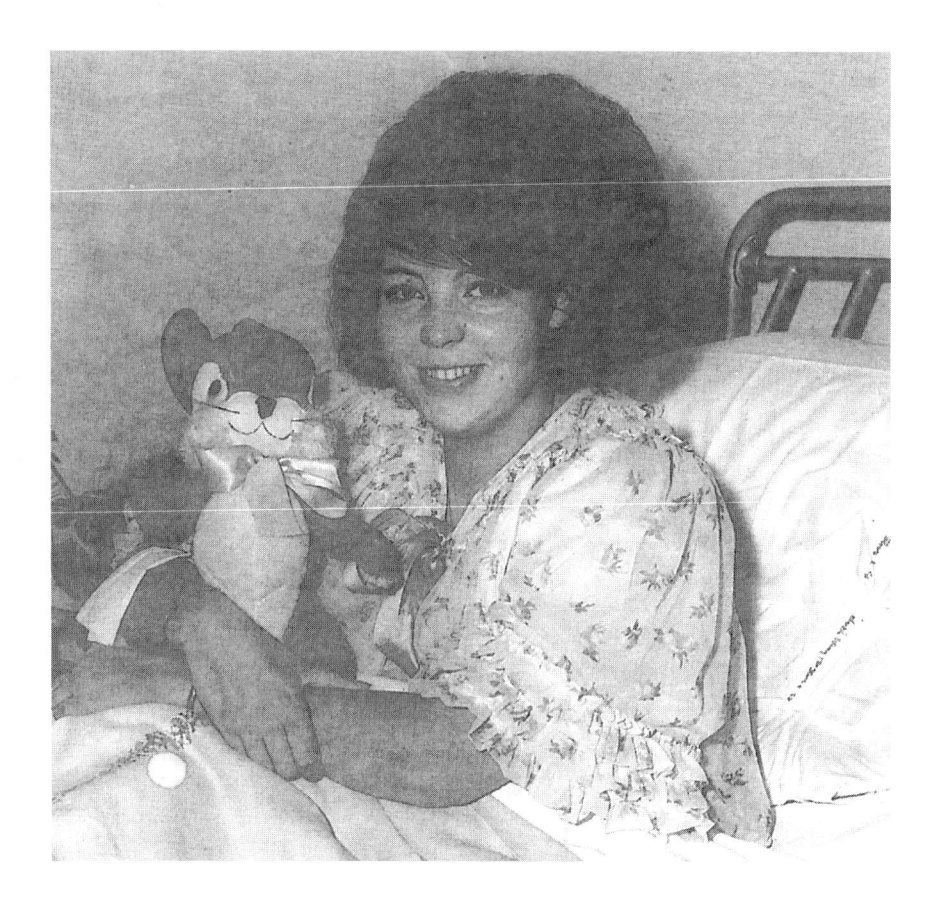

Gordon Coombs was asked by the family to go to the wreck where it lay awash offshore and to retrieve some personal items. They also informed him that they never wanted to see that boat again and rather than have it salvaged, wanted it destroyed. Jimmy Webster is a skilled diver and an explosives expert. As it happened he was at that time engaged by the States of Jersey Harbours Department to remove by explosives certain off lying rocks near the entrance to St Helier Harbour.

Jimmy agreed to accompany Gordon on his mission and they used Jimmy's workboat. They moored alongside the remains of the 'Maricelia' and Jimmy dived. Having retrieved the items requested, as agreed with Gordon, he then placed explosive charges inside the hull and set the fuses. Even now the 'Maricelia' was to hold out another surprise, for as Jimmy hauled himself back over the side of his boat weighed down by his diving gear and Gordon went to start up the engine, it refused to start!

After several anxious moments the engine responded and just as they cleared the wreck the fuses ignited the explosives and nearly took the propeller off the boat. That was the end of a fine yacht which had carried a family to destruction in the most terrible of sea conditions.

JONQUIL

There is a great thrill, for those who love sailing, in taking delivery of a new yacht. The 'yard itself is full of the smells of hardwoods, glues, paint and many other materials used in its construction. The workforce is often made up of interesting characters you would have to go a long way to find in another regime. I particularly enjoy the good natured banter and soft accents of the south coast. Skilled men and women who have a natural affinity for their craft and who take delight in the perfection of their handiwork.

Austen Janes was a former mining engineer who had operated a mine in Nigeria before 1939. He was a highly intelligent man with a great sense of humour and a fine singing voice. He had become a millionaire quite by chance. His African mining operation consisted of digging up vast quantities of rock and soil which was then vibrated in giant machines to separate out the mineral he sought. Native labour was used to sort the material and conveyor belts built up towering hills of 'spoil', that is the useless waste material.

With the start of the war in Europe, government analysts arrived at all mines to increase efficiency and to determine what

Jonquil

other useful chemicals or ores may be found in the mine. An American team of analysts arrived at Austen's mine and found that his 'spoil' heaps contained rich deposits of columbite which was in high demand for the production of steel used in armour plating. Austen received millions of pounds for his hills of waste material so he sold up and when Nigeria gained its independence, he and Mary his wife came to Jersey to live.

It was Yvonne's mother and father, Vera and Cecil Chevalier and her brother John, who befriended the newly arrived Janes family for they had a son too, 'young' Austen. Soon the two families were on regular visiting terms and took motoring holidays together. Austen decided that he would have a new motoryacht built and chose Frederick Parker to design it. 'Jonquil' was the name chosen for her by Mary Janes and soon the sixty foot long hull was being constructed at Woodnutt's 'yard on the Isle of Wight. The day of her launch came and Austen invited me to accompany him to take delivery of her together with his son who was now sixteen.

It was a beautiful morning when we arrived at Woodnutt's and 'Jonquil' gleamed as her varnish work and fresh paint reflected the low sunlight. It had been decided that she should go immediately to the Hamble River a short distance away for her acceptance trials. This was of course to check her performance and handling. A measured mile was available at Warsash and this was where we picked up a mooring. The trials were not entirely satisfactory and I noticed that the 'yard manager snapped his stopwatch shut without comment after we had run the measured mile and the surveyor who was conducting the trials made his own notes. Later it transpired that 'Jonquil', designed to achieve twelve knots, was barely reaching eight knots and burying her stern while raising her bow so steeply that it was difficult to see forward.

Whatever went on between the parties I was not aware of, but Austen, no doubt dazzled by his new 'toy' accepted her. Now began the work of completing the fitting out. There was so much gear to be brought aboard. There was all the yacht's equipment from lifejackets to handbearing compasses and our own personal gear. It was now that I discovered the awkward relationship between Austen and his son.

I could never quite fathom what went on between them. I was very used to boys of young Austen's age and believed I knew how to get the best out of them. Austen kept his son at arm's length and would not allow him to touch anything. After a while, seeing that the boy was very bored, I said to Austen that I thought young Austen could get the yacht's dinghy and prepare it for use together with its outboard motor. I suggested this because the new dinghy and all its gear lay ashore in a shed and the boy would not be too close to be chivvied and corrected. Reluctantly Austen, who was very busy indeed, agreed. I went ashore with young Austen and soon he was as happy as a lark with the men in the shed taking him under their wing as he looked for tools and other things. He was such a likable and good looking boy that his relationship with his Dad really surprised me. I Supposed, perhaps wrongly, that Austen senior's life in the African bush had ill prepared him for a close relationship with his son.

The new dinghy with a happy young Austen at the helm was soon plying back and forth between the shore and 'Jonquil'. It had been decided that we should sleep aboard and the

Jonquil

accommodation was first class, but the newly installed central heating system began to misbehave. It ran off the supply of fuel oil in the yacht's tanks and began to smoke out the cabins with a heavy smell of diesel fumes. The unit was switched off and the interior ventilated, but the night was bitterly cold on the moorings in the middle of the river, so cold that we could not sleep despite gathering up every sort of covering, for there was no bedding aboard. On examination it turned out that the Webasto central heating unit had been wrongly installed; it would seem that the exhaust had been ducted to the interior of the yacht and the clean hot air to the outside!

The Royal Air Force's Sailing Association Yacht Club was on the opposite river bank to the 'yard and Austen found accommodation for us there. After another day's work, we repaired to our newly found sleeping quarters where we shared one large room. No one had told Austen that it was also a corridor and he sat bolt upright in bed as a young Womens' Royal Air Force Officer opened the door and walked right through wishing us all a good night as she passed. Austen's face said it all, "What next!"

To sort out the heating system and other problems we moved back to Woodnutts' 'yard at Bembridge where we spent a day or two. Austen now planned his departure for Jersey and spent some time at the chart table calculating tides and courses for our homeward journey. He invited me to check his course and after some few minutes I asked him why he was leaving in the late afternoon. "Because the tides serves us best then," he replied. I pointed out to him that it was true that the tides were right for us at 14.00 hrs, but they were equally good at 03.00. Instead of sailing into darkness as we crossed the busy shipping lanes of the English Channel, we would be sailing from dawn and have the whole day of sunlight and good visibility with us. Furthermore his plan meant that we would arrive off Guernsey in the middle of the night. Austen agreed immediately and we turned in early, with the central heating now working, for a start at dawn.

It was a lovely morning and the east coast of the Isle of Wight was bathed in the morning sunlight as we passed it down our starboard side. The two powerful Caterpillar motors were purring quietly below decks. Later off St Catherine's Point, Austen asked me to take the wheel. He was excellent company and as happy as a little boy with his new boat. "I am going to cook you the best breakfast you have ever had," he chuckled after I had been steering 'Jonquil' for the best part of and hour. Down below he went leaving me on the flying bridge with young Austen. The boy had been an excellent crew aboard 'Lalun' my Dragon class yacht, so it was natural that I stood back from the wheel and waved Austen to try his hand. His face lit up and he steered the yacht as well as I knew he would while I stood alongside him 'just in case'. We chatted happily for perhaps twenty minutes when suddenly Austen Senior's head emerged through a nearby hatch. "What are you doing son. Now be careful, can you manage?" The boy turned away from the wheel and walked away.

After what was indeed a memorable breakfast, we ploughed on and soon found ourselves surrounded by many long wooden logs. They were too short to be telegraph poles so we assumed that they were pit props. They must have been a deck cargo which had washed off some cargo ship. As Austen spun the wheel this way and that to avoid colliding with them, we congratulated ourselves on making the trip in the daylight hours. Had we collided at even our slow eight knots with one of them, the resulting damage could have at least disabled 'Jonquil' and might even have sunk her.

It was one of those special mornings where it was so good to be alive. The yacht was new and perfect and we were all happily enjoying the cruise down to Jersey some eight hours away. What could go wrong? Austen, at the wheel, noticed that the port Caterpillar engine was losing revolutions, the gauge was falling back slowly, steadily, minute by minute. The twin engines had lost that synchronous beat that the human ear can detect so well and were now sounding definitely uncomfortable. Our less than generous speed was dropping too, seven then six knots. The high bow fell to a lower angle. I took the wheel while Austen visited the engine room and checked around. We now noticed that the port engine was beginning to overheat. What could have caused this problem? One moment we were cruising along without a care, the next we had a serious problem. This could not be happening to a new yacht with the very best of engines.

Our course was now recalculated for five knots and the Jersey arrival time moved significantly away from our original target. Thank goodness we had left at dawn and had daylight to consider our position. Austen shut down the port engine and I found 'Jonquil' now difficult to steer. We would still make Jersey at a reasonable time, but we did not need any more trouble.

However, we soon got more trouble. "Austen, the starboard engine is losing revolutions now." Austen could not believe it, but sure enough, the revolution counter was falling back minute by minute just as the port engine had done. We were just entering the Little Roussel channel intending to sail down past Guernsey and on to Jersey, but now we deemed it necessary to enter St Peter Port harbour; if we could make it that far. The engine set us back to three knots and repeated the slow temperature rise of the other one. Fortunately the tide was still with us and we edged our way into the outer harbour where Austen intended to anchor as manoeuvring on one engine to pick up a mooring buoy was going to be difficult to put it mildly. Just as you might now expect, 'Jonquils' hydraulic winch powered by our 'sick' engine refused to lower the anchor and had to be disconnected while the chain was manhandled over the bow.

Using our dinghy we soon had an engineer aboard. Eventually he diagnosed fuel problems and settled on the diesel fuel filters as the problem. The wrong ones had been fitted and had very gradually passed less and less fuel to the engines. With new filters fitted, an hour or two later we were back at sea running down towards St Helier in fine style, while Austen considered what he was going to say to Woodnutt's 'yard on the telephone in the morning.

Some months later Austen asked me if I would 'con' 'Jonquil' through the 'gutters' to Gorey. The 'gutters' was a route to the lovely east coast harbour of Gorey, but instead of heading out to sea from St Helier and circling the enormous reef of rocks which lie to the south east of Jersey one merely went through the reef. I had been taught the tricky route by my good friend Bob Kempster and its directions were amusing. You relied upon identifying large rocks, 'heads' the old fishermen called them, and transits inland. The instructions included charming pieces of information such as to line up the second dormer window on 'Bramble Cottage' with the pierhead light or close the wall on La Rocque slipway with half of the mark on the wall 'where the lifebelt used to be!' Bob had chuckled with glee as he had witnessed my disbelief at some of the marks.

I had used the passage several times and it cut the time to Gorey considerably. So one fine morning in perfect conditions Austen and I set off in 'Jonquil' for Gorey by the Inner Passage or 'gutters'. Austen gave me the helm and he soon became very very quiet glancing at his chart and listening intently as I called out the marks to him and turned this way and that on quite a safe route to Gorey, IF you knew it. We had reached the middle of the route and I was just running down towards a grand head of Jersey's best granite when Austen lost his cool. "Stop the boat, Leo," he shouted and looked very agitated. One of the factors on this run was tidal depth and currents and we were well committed to our passage, so I told Austen that we could not stop.

Had I put the engines into neutral we would in fact not have stopped at all, but would have drifted at the mercy of the currents around us. He was white, but took my advice and I now knew that he would be in a state until we emerged safely at the Gorey end of the 'gutters'. Which we did. Austen was so apologetic and I fully understood how he felt. His lovely new yacht had been deep inside some of the most notorious reefs and gullies anywhere. Looking back, I could not do it now for I have forgotten the transits, but I think I was foolish to take a sixty foot yacht through. However, she must have made a grand sight as she turned and headed this way and that deep within the reefs and I still smile a little secret smile to myself when I think back to it.

Austen took Yvonne's mother and father on several visits to the Brittany coast and Mary Janes accompanied them. By all accounts 'Jonquil' was a comfortable and seaworthy motoryacht. Austen employed a crew member to assist him occasionally. At one time he used to bring his gardener down, but when the shipyard 'lads' cottoned on to that they used to say, "They'll soon be growing geraniums out of the portholes." Austen decided to sell 'Jonquil', I think he wanted a break from yachting. So it was that this lovely yacht was sold to an English owner and soon left Jersey for good.

Austen was sitting in the sunshine on the doorstep of the South Pier Shipyard brokerage office as I happened to pass by. He looked up at me with a wistful, but dazed look; I thought perhaps he was not feeling well. "I say, Leo," he murmured in his clipped and unmistakable public school accent, "I've just bought *Eve of Arun*." He grinned happily up at me squinting into the bright sunlight to gauge my reaction. I was surprised, but congratulated him on his purchase.

Fred Scott, 'Eve of Arun's' previous owner who had recently purchased her from George Seymour stood nearby and he confirmed the deal. Fred was a motor dealer who ran quite a large showroom in St Helier together with his partner Peter Gatehouse. In the layout of his business and in his own attitude he was 'ahead of the game' and made the other dealers seem old-fashioned. I had bought one or two cars from him. Practically his first sale in Jersey had been a lovely little Sunbeam-Talbot 10 sports saloon he had sold to me one very wet winter night. On the demonstration drive the car had misfired badly and I remember Freddie stopping the car in the pouring rain outside Goldsmith's Garage on Victoria Avenue, right next to the Millbrook Coronation Park. He scampered inside leaving me sitting in the passenger seat, the rain sluiced off his leather jerkin, but he emerged proudly with four new sparkplugs and a socket spanner. He soon changed the plugs and the car ran well. One hundred and twenty pounds changed hands and the sale was completed.

'Eve of 'Arun' was much admired in local waters. She ran well at sea and was very well fitted out. I recall being surprised to see that she even had spare propellers carefully mounted up near the engine room. She suited Austen far better than 'Jonquil'.

One morning when the tide was out I was standing on the beach in the Old Harbour with Gordon Coombs who was skippering 'Eve' for Austen. The yacht was dried out on the blocks for attention to the underwater area. She shone in the morning sunshine and prompted me to say to Gordon how proud owners must feel of their fine yachts when they see them like this. Gordon moved his pipe in his mouth and, employing a few colourful adjectives which I have left out, said, "Y'know Leo, they're all so busy worrying about their stocks and shares and the price of gold that they never give it a minute's thought." From that time I began to understand that the bigger the yacht, the more expensive it is, the more items of equipment you have on board, the less pleasure you can get from it. The real pleasure in sailing is sail. Sailing a small yacht quietly along using the minimum of distracting extra gear is the essence of the sport.

Austen must have felt this for he came out sailing with me and we accompanied him to Guernsey on one occasion. We sailed across in our Dragon, 'Lalun'. We left ahead of 'Eve of Arun' and he caught up with us halfway across having left Jersey much later. Yvonne and I had invited young Austen to sail with us and he had willingly agreed. Now Yvonne and Austen were scampering around the long narrow deck trimming the little yacht and just enjoying life. Young Austen was a perfect crew member, I remember how neatly he stowed away the sails and made mats of the rope tails around the deck as we moored alongside 'Eve of Arun' in St Peter Port Harbour. Another perfect day, just one of many.

Austen sold 'Eve of Arun' to buy a new motoryacht, half her size at twenty-eight feet overall. The 'Royal Cruisers' were Swedish built craft of high quality with twin diesel engine installations. They were delivered from Sweden to Southampton as deck cargo on ships and offloaded to a shipyard there. It seemed a good adventure for Austen to buy one of these expensive little craft, half the size of his previous yacht, and to sail it across to Jersey on his own.

All went well and Austen was very happy with his new motoryacht as it soared towards the Channel Islands at twice the speed of his previous yachts. He sat at the wheel feeling the rush of the wind past his head and the thrill of driving this willing little mount. Hello, was that a spot of rain? Austen stopped to raise the beautifully fitted, blue canvas canopy with its clear windows. He resumed his course and off he shot. That's funny he thought after and hour or two with light rain falling around him. Should have seen the Casquets by now. He motored on. At last, out of the slight haze brought up with the rain, he saw some high dunes and cliffs ahead of him. This was definitely not right! He stopped to consider his position. Could the compass be wrong? Had not it been 'swung' by the 'yard'. Yes, they had even given him the Correction Card. Hold on a moment. He lowered the steel frame of the canvas hood watching the compass as he did so. It gently rotated back to another position many degrees different from the one he had been using for the last hour or two.

He motored slowly forward to look for an identifiable landmark. There was someone swimming. He motored gently up to him. "Excusez-moi, Monsieur." It transpired that Austen was not far from Cherbourg and a long way off course. All's well that ends well. He was soon zooming down towards Jersey, but by quite a different route.

Austen gave up sailing eventually as Mary his wife began to have rheumatic problems and could no longer cope with steps and boarding boats and dinghies. Undaunted, Austen bought a huge Winnebago camper van and they cruised Europe together. As ever this big vehicle had to be modified to suit Austen's needs and he decided to tow a Mini behind it for use when the camper van was parked on a site. A fairground owner of Austen's acquaintance had told him that they towed vehicles such as cars behind their vans by means of a special tow bar and that no trailer was required. The tow bar was made up at a local engineering workshop and I found myself one day sitting behind the steering wheel of the Mini while Austen drove the Winnebago round the Island roads.

The Mini's steering wheel spun this way and that as it followed the towing vehicle just as though a driver had his hands on the wheel. Very impressive. Austen was pleased, although he did later discover that the front tires wore rather too quickly. We did not see much of Austen around the yacht club and harbours after this time, to our loss. He was an interesting and likable man.

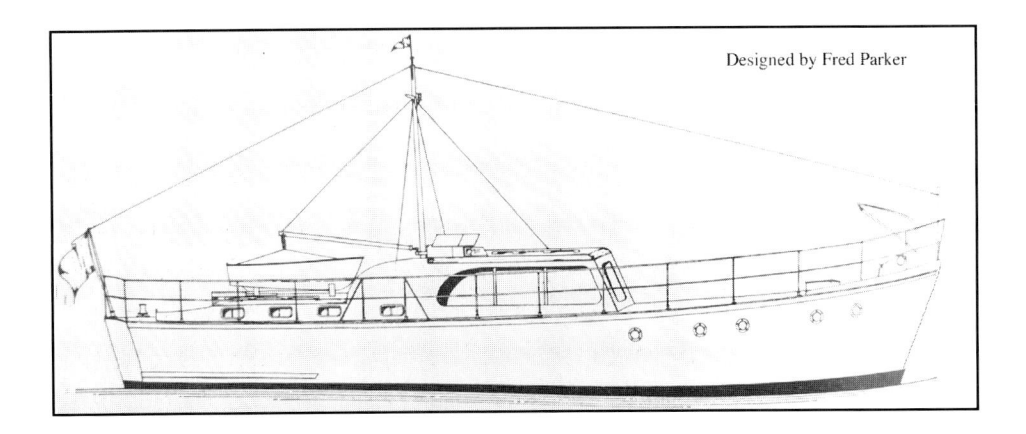

Designed by Fred Parker

THE GAFFERS

Gaff rigged yachts were a common sight in Jersey waters in the 1950's, this was the old rig of a former era. The Bermudan rig was rapidly overhauling it in popularity for it was not only much simpler and therefore cheaper to install on a yacht, but it was much more efficient to windward. Off the wind, reaching and downwind it was another matter, the gaff rigged yacht often still held her own. But forget the efficiency and look at the pleasure which handling a gaffer gave her crew. They were a delight to the eye as they swept majestically along under full sail with topsails trimmed to a fresh breeze and the square mainsail full of power, supported by a pair of overlapping jibs hiding the long bowsprit. Could anything have spoken more clearly of the story and power of sail.

It was as though these fine vessels imparted something of their own character to their owners and crews who seemed very relaxed and contented with their lovely old yachts. 'Taquah', 'Onyx', 'Marguerite' and several others were all of this ilk and had been working craft before their conversion to yachts. 'Onyx' had been built in 1849 and began life as a fishing boat as had 'Taquah', while the much larger 'Marguerite' had been a Bristol pilot cutter. But let me tell you just a little about them.

Dudley Harrison was the owner of 'Taquah', a gentle man, softly spoken and with a ready smile and balancing sense of humour. His round glasses echoed his rounded features and stayed on his nose despite every sort of effort to dislodge them whether it be a flick from a tarred line or a brush with the canvas of a jib. He hurried around his lovely charge tightening halliards and easing jibs to return to his place at the wheel. The wheel itself was a characterful affair, spoked and bound in brass, it was quite small and strangely positioned, for the helmsman had to stand with his back to it as there was no room to stand either alongside or behind it. It came off the end of a manufactured steering gear system consisting of worm gears and clever geometric arms which directly turned the head of the large, heavy rudder mounted so squarely on the transom. But....beware your fingers and clothes as the heavily greased exposed moving parts churned relentlessly back and forward in answer to the movements of the wheel.

Everything about 'Taquah' spoke of durability and fitness for seagoing purpose. All her gear whether it was anchor or mainsail boom was heavy and took some effort to handle and she sailed powerfully, often showing a clean transom to a little racing squadron. My introduction to 'Taquah' and to Dudley was as ever through my brother Francis, who had become friendly with him before I had joined St Helier Yacht Club. Dudley had been looking for crew and Francis 'offered' me. According to Francis, Dudley was not too keen to take an absolute rookie aboard, but eventually agreed to give me a try.

The first sail I recall with Dudley and 'Taquah' was to Chausey, those then delightful Breton islands just twenty miles away to the south. We were to leave the inner harbour at about four in the morning. I arrived by car to the bright lights of the quay complete with a small kitbag for a weekend sail. The tide was out, but rising and the yachts lay in the glistening mud of their moorings, everything was so quiet, the silence only broken by the sound of some seabird or the scuttle of a rat. Dudley was there wearing Wellingtons and quickly pointed out that my sailing shoes were not very suitable for the 'walk' through the mud out to 'Taquah' as he intended to be aboard her before she floated and did not want to leave his dinghy on the mooring. Plan 'B' was soon implemented and as with all plan 'Bs' it proved to be not too brilliant. Dudley climbed down the long vertical wooden ladder fixed to the huge old granite stones of the pier and I followed to be 'piggybacked' out to the waiting boat. How daft can you be? Of course as I got onto Dudley's shoulders he slipped, through my sudden arrival and we both fell into the mud!

Unfortunately the palm of my right hand encountered a piece of sharp glass and came up bleeding through thick mud and an obvious case for the Emergency Department at the General Hospital. Dudley whisked me round in his little 'Y' series M.G. saloon and an hour or so later, with my hand bandaged, we were aboard 'Taquah'. I still have the scar to remind me of this.

The heavy cruising yacht was a new experience for me, as she made light of the small seas which were running, plunging her stemhead and bowsprit at regular intervals and tossing spray across her foredeck. The decks ran with seawater and had that look of well-washed wood and clean simplicity, where everything had a purpose and was well fastened down. It was a pleasure to be with Dudley and his regular crew and soon we ran into the Sound at Chausey from the south. It was early on a

Lee Ho

The Gaffers

beautiful Saturday morning with small, colourful fishing boats bobbing around us and a delightful island beyond. Soon the smell of frying bacon permeated 'Taquah' and later we launched the dinghy and all four of us headed for the nearby shore leaving 'Taquah' well moored in a little bay just below an old chapel. We had fitted her legs so that as the tide dropped and she grounded on the beach she would stand upright. Nothing is less comfortable than being aboard a grounded yacht when she is lying on her side.

How can I best describe the pure, innocent pleasure of wandering around an unknown island, visiting little bays on foot and examining old wrecks and occasionally catching a distant view through the trees and shrubs of your little white yacht gently swinging in a light breeze. It is complete contentment, especially in the company of good friends.

Then there was the café with its French atmosphere and plentiful supply of beer and good wines. Later in the day we stood on the beach looking up at 'Taquah' and waiting to climb up her port leg in turns using the wedgelike wooden steps fastened to it.

Lunch aboard was in the white painted cabin sitting round a varnished table with complete informality. Everything is within easy reach and the atmosphere is relaxed and good humoured. After lunch, perhaps a little snooze or swim in the clear water or a gentle stroll to a nearby farm where the farmer's wife sells you the most beautiful butter to take home.

We sleep well as the yacht gently lifts off the beach on the rising tide and on Sunday morning we are making ready to leave at mid day for the sail back to Jersey. 'Taquah' heels to a gentle breeze and her big mainsail and topsail curve as though made of thin carved wood and the sea chuckles past her stern quarter. The distant view of the Islands bathed in sunlight is restful and inviting. This is sailing!

Dudley was keen to race 'Taquah' in the club's handicap events in which she did quite well. However, in chatting with Captain Ronnie Taylor about sailing a gaff rigged yacht, he told me that the one big secret about making a gaffer sail was to "ease her off and," he said, "when you think you have eased her off enough, ease her some more." By this he meant that the big square mainsail should be let out on its sheet and not sailed like a Bermudan rig. My chance to try this out came on a race from St Helier to St Malo. We started quite well and were soon following 'Julietta' a quite new Burmudan rigged yacht owned by Lester Le Sueur. Andy, a shipyard carpenter and an excellent helmsman was sailing her in the light breeze and 'Taquah' trundled along behind with me at the helm.

It was obvious to Dudley that this would be the position for a long time with 'Julietta' steadily drawing away from us. He went below to attend to the navigation as we cleared the Demie des Pas tower and I had the wheel. I began to ease the mainsheet from where it had been set and noticed little difference to our speed. I eased it more until it was almost hanging loose and watched and waited. There was a different feel to her and gradually we began to overtake the leading yacht. Dudley came up to see what I had been up to and thought that we must be carrying a breeze up with us towards the leader.

The Gaffers

Our long bowsprit was getting uncomfortably close to the stern of 'Julietta' when Andy, alone at the helm, suddenly became aware of our challenge and began to adjust his sheets and to become active about the boat. His crew came up from their lunch and looked at us as we gently passed to leeward, the smaller modern rig of their yacht hardly affecting the large spread of 'Taquahs' canvas. It was not to last; after an hour or so, the wind freshened and swung round more onto our bow and gave our gaff rig the point of sailing into the wind where it is least efficient.

Off the wind in a fresh breeze the gaffers took a lot of beating and often placed well in races where the conditions suited them. It was wonderful to be aboard them then, with their towering canvas and to feel the thrust and power as they breasted the waves and thrust their bowsprit and jibs into the sea. They trembled beneath your feet and shook their masts and rigging as they responded to the wind and sea. They were 'wet' boats, spray and small waves of seawater rushed across their decks, but they were a thrill to sail and a lot of work to maintain and to use.

'Onyx' was the oldest gaffer, dating back to the 1800's. She too had started life as a fishing boat on the southwest coast. Converted to a comfortable yacht, she had come into the possession of Graham Godfray, a keen yachtsman and a great character. He was one of a special breed of men, men of few words who carry a presence with them and seem to influence matters by their mere attendance. He was quite tall and well-built with a slight stoop as though living too long below decks had induced this stance. Graham had a strong sense of humour and a ready laugh, but was often lost in concentration and consideration of some more serious point. He sailed 'Onyx' with great élan and performed well in club events, usually at his best in long distance racing.

Graham went on to sail very different yachts, but 'Onyx' now came into the possession of another fine character in the person of Harry Fenn. Harry is ex-navy having served during the 1940's as a sickbay attendant on landing craft and had been present at the invasion of Normandy in 1944. Harry sailed 'Onyx' in many club races and maintained her good record until he too was 'weaned' into buying a lovely steel Dutch built 'Trintel' class yacht, 'Zaria'. But, before that Harry and 'Onyx' became a regular feature on the yachting scene.

I remember so well coming out of Granville on a windy Sunday morning late in the season with some members of our football team aboard 'Dancing Lady'. A big sea was running just outside the harbour walls as we left, well reefed. I was following 'Onyx' about fifty to one hundred feet astern of her when she started to climb the face of a large sea while 'Dancing Lady' descended the opposite face. I can clearly recall looking down from my high vantage point onto 'Onyxs' mast head and saw her complete deckplan from bowsprit to rudder laid out before me. I thought that we were going to accelerate down the face of our wave and collide with her stern, but in the way of these things, we slowed up as the wave passed under us. Later on we were sailing across Grouville Bay alongside 'Onyx', watching her long bowsprit plunging deep beneath the waves and running along like a shark or dolphin before rising up with seawater cascading off every part of the bow and jibs. Powerful, but wet were the gaffers.

Is that the end of the gaffers. I think not. Wherever one can be found they are being restored to their former glory and the unmistakable silhouette can often be seen. 'Onyx' waits, as I write, for restoration by the Jersey Maritime Museum team of craftsmen who have already restored at least three of these fine craft.

THE MARGUERITE

Bristol Pilot Cutters were the epitome of the true 'Gaffer'. Huge, by our standards, at sixty feet overall they were designed to lie off Bristol in the Severn Estuary and await 'trade'. 'Trade' was sailing and later steam ships approaching the port and in need of a pilot to con them in. Several pilots would board her and set her huge gaff and jibs for the open sea where they would watch out for the signal pennant and another job to guide some ship's master in to a secure berth.

It was said that when the last pilot had been put aboard a ship by use of the cutter's heavy dinghy, the 'boy' (read young man, possibly apprentice pilot) would row back to the cutter where she lay in 'stays' with one sail counteracting another so that she stood relatively still in the sea. Once aboard he would attach a ready prepared strop from the boom to hooks on the dinghy, then let fly the jib. The cutter would gather way and the 'boy' would then throw over the helm so that the boom swept over the deck and as it reached the centre of the aft deck the strop was jerked to drop the dinghy neatly onto its chocks. An enjoyable sail home then ensued.

The Marguerite

However that may be, the boom was enormous extending well out over the vessel's stern and was often a solid piece of spruce. You can imagine what may happen if ever this hefty item got out of control. It could sweep the aft deck from side to side providing a nasty shock for anyone who got in its way. Great care was needed in handling it and a gybe was almost unforgivable.

At the other end of the cutter was another formidable hunk of wood, the bowsprit. On this piece of well chosen timber depended the security of the mast, sails and all the great mass of rigging. It was fastened down to the bow by a strong chain and to improve the angle of the chain, was fitted over a sturdy piece of iron which started from under the midpoint of the boom. This downward pointing piece of ironwork was often referred to as 'the dolphin striker' for reasons which require little explanation. The bowsprit itself earned the name 'the widow maker', for if you fell off while handling a heavy, wet, canvas jib or, more likely you were knocked off by a sudden flap of the sail, you stood little chance of surviving contact with the fast moving bow and your passage under the hull. Come to that, it was impossible for a large sailing ship to heave to and pick a person out of the sea. Miles may have passed before a boat could be readied and launched and the chance of spotting a crewman's head in the vast expanse would be minimal.

Back to the bowsprit and 'The Marguerite'. Terry Ashborn had enjoyed a pleasant sail down to St Malo from Jersey and now they lay alongside the quay in the Bassin Vauban, the non tidal harbour approached through a lock. Then the two left aboard as the watch were asked if they could move to another position further along the quay past some other moored vessels.

Terry and his partner decided that they could move 'Marguerite' without more help and so cast off. Most single engined sailing craft do not handle well under auxiliary power when going astern and this 'yacht' was no different, so they took her out of her berth by going ahead. This part of the task well done they then headed back up the quay to their new berth. Terry could never understand why the man on the helm decided to turn 'Marguerite' around to lie the same way as she had been when all they had to do was to slip into the berth and tie up. But no, round came her head and so too that long, long bowsprit and Terry standing in the bow could see that it would sweep the walkway along the quay and the cars parked facing the moored boats. He shouted back to the helmsman to go astern and clambered along the traversing 'sprit shouting to clear the idle onlookers and dropped to the quay in a gallant attempt to prevent some hapless Citroen or Renault from being impaled. There was little possibility of stopping the disaster now looming, but Terry pushed the balk of timber back and along, jumping over bumpers and other motoring paraphernalia until the bowsprit cleared the quay and the danger was past. Perhaps the engine running full astern had saved the day and combined with Terry's efforts had prevented serious damage. Whatever, the recollection of the event was like recalling a nightmare.

Terry also had another interesting adventure aboard 'Marguerite'. On quite another occasion, they had left St Malo for the trip up to Jersey when the wind, which had been light, dropped away completely. The engine was started and they continued under power. After some time sitting in the cockpit yarning with the crew, Terry went down below to find his camera or some such errand. His foot now resting on the carpet 'sank' and the carpet folded upwards like a daffodil around his

The Marguerite

swamped deck shoe. "We have sprung a leak. Man the pump," he shouted. Soon the pump was clanking away and buckets of water were passed up by hand from the large saloon. The water gained on their efforts and 'Marguerite' was in danger. They swung around to nearby St Malo and opened the throttle wide, to enter the outer harbour and tie alongside with deep water throughout the hull and a very sluggish boat under them. Floors were lifted to look for the leak and there it was. The hosepipe for the engine cooling water from the engine to the sea had become detached and was happily emptying the contents of the harbour into the hull by means of the cooling pump. The faster they had run the engine, the more had they swamped their boat!

At last 'Marguerite' was sold and came into the ownership of an American lady, one 'Pumphandle' Lou. Why 'Pumphandle'? Well you see, the old fashioned pump on board 'Marguerite' was worked by a detachable oak handle of about the size of a baseball bat. Now the said 'Pumphandle' Lou was a powerful woman who knew her own mind and stood for no nonsense. When it was drawn to her attention that a certain 'hanger on' around the South Pier, a man, what we would call a paedophile today, had been showing interest in her young boy, she seized the nearest thing to hand, yes, you are quite right, the pumphandle and went looking for him all in one wintry night. I cannot satisfy your curiosity by telling you if she ever found him, but I think not. A wise man would have caught the earliest available 'mailboat' off the Island. However, the nickname stuck and I will always associate the lovely 'Marguerite' with 'Pumphandle' Lou.

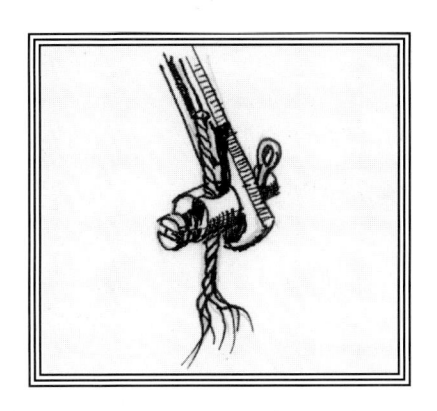

REMEMBER, IT'S ONLY A BIT OF WIRE

This chapter relates to sailing yachts when under engine power and to all motor powered craft. You move the gear control lever confidently from neutral to ahead and back to neutral, pause and then astern so frequently and all is well. Have you ever considered what may happen if things do not go as you planned? One or two salutary reminders to check everything and to keep up the maintenance can be found in the following!

Brian Slous hired a riverboat of around forty feet overall, he had as his 'crew' a group of secondary children of 16 years old, both boys and girls. He was a very experienced teacher, a competent sailor and was both quick and active as his sporting prowess exemplified. The locks on the Breton canals are quite small and narrow and very picturesque, often situated in the countryside with floral gardens tended by the lockeeper and his family. Fortunately Brian had been able to admire them very often, because what I am about to relate rather spoiled the enjoyment of the latest lock he was about to enter.

The lock was not quite ready when he arrived outside it and he had to wait as the sluices were operated on the closed lock gates. Still, what did it matter, the weather was fine, the birds were singing, all was going well and the 'crew' was happy. The boat drifted off line while waiting and would have to be manoeuvred a bit before it could enter the lock. Moored against the nearby quay was a smaller French yacht with children on her deck, amusing themselves and enjoying the warm weather. The large tarred, wooden gates made of massive timber had their own habitat of selected river weeds caught in the cracks and joints of the structure. Dribbles and even small jets of water forced through the gate by the great pressure within and made pleasant noises as they fell down into the still green water. Suddenly the water began to seethe and boil as the sluices in the gate were opened and continued until a current of swirling water and debris drifted off downriver. At last the gates cracked open letting the last ripple of water and small items of debris whirl slowly by on the river water, now more than a little agitated by the functioning of the lock.

Brian bided his time then slipped his large single engine into ahead and finding himself at an angle to the correct line to enter moved the gearlever from ahead to neutral, paused correctly and then went astern. The boat responded and after a momentary hesitation while the propeller dug in, slid back slowly to give more manoeuvring room, Brian spun his wheel and brought the gearlever through neutral – pause – and then ahead, but gave the motor some 'welly' to throw a cascade of water from the propeller against the angled rudder while he watched ahead for the bow to swing into its correct line for the lock. But....what was this? The bow seemed to be held and not lining up, more throttle! Brian gave the engine more throttle and then, only then it seemed that the bow moved, but not as intended, it was not swinging into line, but retreating from the open lock. There was only one thing to do. He gave the engine full throttle to stop the boat!

Somewhere beneath his feet the gremlins had been at work and the cable operating the gearbox selector had finally broken when he had engaged astern and the selector was now resting in that position, and no waggling of the gearlever in Brian's now sweating palm was going to change it. With the first burst of throttle the long boat had gathered up her skirts and started astern and now with full throttle was enjoying an unusual full speed astern. Brian glanced sideways out of the wheelhouse window and what he saw made him cut the engine and sent him athletically leaping onto the side deck and pounding aft as fast as he could go. The boat was heading fast towards the quay he had just left and straight for the French yacht on which the children lingered quite unaware of the impending accident. There was no way to avoid a collision. He shouted and waved. His own 'crew' could not understand what was wrong and as he neared the French yacht he slid down onto the deck at the stern and held out his foot in an attempt to fend it off.

Contact was made at some speed, but Brian's ankle could not take such a strain and broke, the yacht rolled over, but did not sink and the riverboat came to a shuddering halt, both boats sustaining some superficial damage. There was of course much crying, shouting and tears and raised voices, but after some time, at last peace was restored and the ambulance came. Other school staff aboard the riverboat, retrieved the situation and pacified all and sundry. This was all down to the snapping of a piece of bowden cable a little thicker than a pencil lead. Have you thought about yours lately?

On a less serious level; when Dudley first owned 'Taquah', the heavy gaff yacht I have already described, she was fitted with a 'converted' Fordson tractor engine. It was 'converted' but only in as far as it had been lifted out of the tractor and dropped into 'Taquah'. The original massive gearlever of the tractor emerged from the cockpit sole and was used to achieve neutral, ahead and astern, other gears were considered, but thought unnecessary and thus never employed. What amused me most was that the clutch pedal also protruding from the sole, had too been found unnecessary!

In a moment of financial madness, Dudley was offered and bought a nice, second-hand, four cylinder, diesel Mercedes marine engine. There was no clutch pedal when it was finally fitted and the gearlever became a neat little stick placed conveniently beside the tiller. All seemed well.

I was plodding across St Aubins Bay in 'Dancing Lady' one fine summer afternoon to enjoy a family day out, anchored off a nearby beach, when we saw 'Taquah' under tow. She was headed for St Helier Harbour as we turned and headed to cross her course and to enquire what was wrong. "The engine won't start, I have tried everything," Dudley told us. After a few more words, Dudley dropped the tow with thanks and we took over, resuming our course for the beach.

With both yachts at anchor I asked Dudley if I could have a look at his engine, Dudley offered no resistance, he was properly fed up. I did not attempt to start it up, as this had been tried already and starter motors can soon flatten a battery. Instead I lifted the cockpit sole to see what may appear. After a few minutes I spotted the problem. Yes, you have guessed it, a broken cable, but this time to the fuel cut off lever which stops the diesel engine and, of course, it could not be started without being moved to the 'fuel on' position. I moved the lever with one finger, closed the floor, and started the engine much to Dudley's surprise and obvious pleasure.

I had been asked to crew on a large 'trawler yacht' of 38 feet overall. We took her from Cambrills on the Mediterranean Spanish coast to the Arsenale in central Paris. It was a wonderful trip through the Rhone in mid-winter, January 1990. David, the skipper and the lovely Micky, his wife were excellent company. But….yes, a cable broke as we were coming out of a large lock while running on both engines. The yacht started to turn to starboard as the engine controls were moved. We anchored in a quiet corner and investigated. I soon found that the broken cable affected the selector unit which allowed either the use of the flying bridge controls or the wheelhouse ones. Half-an-hour later and one recycled wire clothes hanger and we were underway using only the wheelhouse single lever controls. It could have been much more serious as we often had to pass heavily laden barges on the river and the suction of their passing by had to be met with judicious use of both engines.

Many years before this, one of the earliest fibreglass hulled yachts came to stay in Jersey for a while. 'Cosmic Breeze' was 30 feet overall and had twin bilge keels and sported an aft cabin. She was terribly simple around the deck compared with our gaffers and lacked character. She was more like an upside down bath than anything. Her owners, the Lawrences, used her frequently and on an extended visit, made many friends in Jersey and joined in with the club's activities.

The nearby Napoleonic canals below St Malo leading into deepest Brittany attracted them and so they took down their mast in St Malo and passing through the Barrage were soon in the River Rance and then after several locks were further inland.

It seems that after moments of deep pleasure, an ensuing tragedy is also felt much more deeply too. The scene could not have been more idyllic as 'The Breeze' neared the open lock filled with still water and with its gates welcoming them and a friendly lock-keeper standing ready at his post. The short aluminium gearlever with its large, black knob nestled in the helmsman's hand as he came confidently into the lock at some speed, some may think too much speed, but who am I to judge, a quick burst astern and the crew would have her stopped and throw their ropes around the nearby bollards.

I would not be writing this now if that was what was to be. You see, this aluminium rod gearlever complete with heavy black knob played its part in engaging the yacht's gearbox by being held down into a shallow hole in an inner shaft when it functioned as a gearlever. If you only wanted to 'rev' the motor you lifted it a little out of this hole and you had no gear movement, only throttle. Are you still with me? Now to go astern and to stop the heavy yacht travelling too quickly towards the far, closed lock gate, towering eight feet above the canal below, you only have to swing the lever towards you backwards. Hey Presto, the yacht steadies reduces speed and stops, but NOT if it has failed to lodge in that little, shallow hole which engages the gearbox and astern. Instead, if it is not engaged as aforementioned, the swinging of the gearlever operates only the throttle and you accelerate in whichever gear you happen to be in!

Remember, It's Only A Bit Of Wire

It happened just like that. Away went the visions of the floral display, the pretty lock and smiling 'keeper'. The yacht hurtled towards the closed lock gate and hit it with such force that the yacht's bow climbed skyward on the tarred oak, clearing away as it did the polite French notices on the use of the locks and certain useful handrails on top of the gates. After a moment or two as the crew regained their feet and the stern glimmered beneath the water the bow slipped back as the helmsman cut the motor. What of the 'keeper'? He was many good French metres away, frightened out of his life and afraid that the lock gate would burst outwards permitting a great deluge of water to thunder down onto the surrounding countryside.

He returned eventually, but not before a good half hour had passed, then he railed and ranted and refused to operate the gate or to allow the yacht to leave until the engineers from far away Rennes had checked it and its mechanism. The 'Breeze' was there for a further day or two before all accounts were settled and she was given permission to go back, well marked and tar blackened and with a much chastened skipper and crew, now not quite so keen on the canals.

This was not so much a broken cable, as a design fault which caused this to happen. It pays to be cautious when handling a yacht at close quarters. If the yacht has locked in the wrong gear, it just does not occur to you for a few precious moments and then you may not be able to remedy the problem. I did design a small three light operating system directly off the gearbox selector lever and sent it up to Morse Controls Ltd, but they did not think it worthwhile. I was surprised, after all a pretty set of green, amber and red lights on his steering console would be every yachtsman's delight. Or could it just save a major problem unfolding?

THE 'COMPLEAT YACHTSMAN'

Gordon Jones hailed from North Wales and was born and brought up around Caernarvon, that lovely historic town with its fine castle overlooking the sea and the river. He became a craftsman par excellence turning his talents to many different media. Silversmith, musical instrument maker to name but two. Above all he was a gifted teacher able to transmit his enthusiasm and deep personal love for his work to his students. Underlying all of this was an interest in sailing which began in his teenage years and became a dream to build his own yacht.

Gordon's career took him to south London and while he was there his brother offered him some larch trees growing on his farm back in Wales. Larch is an excellent boatbuilding timber and very soon the kiln dried planks were awaiting Gordon's hand in a shed on the banks of the river Medway. His love for the sea was now increased by a set of drawings for a lovely little yacht called 'The Clyde Cruising Club One Design' These twenty-eight foot long yachts were to be built along identical specifications and raced against each other without handicap, hence the 'One Design' nomenclature. Clinker planked and with a long cabin they were very pretty and excellent seaboats.

'Gafr Wen', for Gordon chose to name his yacht in his mother tongue after a little white goat which figures in a Welsh folk song, began to take shape in the confines of an old shed. He smiled wryly as he told me of his first 'mistake'. He had discovered an engine for his new yacht. It was the little Stuart Turner, twin cylinder two stroke of ten horsepower. Built at a lovely factory situated on a quiet stretch of the Thames at Henley, its very British craftsmanship and origin appealed to Gordon's sense of perfection. He drove to the factory and bought one..

Now Gordon's cash flow was a problem; recently married to the lovely Sheila he was trying to do what other aspiring yachtsmen have done and will do for evermore, make ends meet while burning the candle at both ends, if you will forgive the mixed but apt metaphor. So the investment of a substantial sum of money in the auxiliary motor before the keel was even laid meant that Gordon's funds were very low indeed. He said to me, "That was a mistake boy. That motor stood there gathering dust in the shed watching me build the boat. I should have used the money it cost to buy a planing machine which would have worked for me and could have been sold when I had finished with it."

One incident Gordon recounted to me showed what craftsmanship existed in boatbuilding of the past. He had visited an old long established firm which used to build barges and other river craft in wood. Chatting with an old man, long since retired, the old fellow asked Gordon what he was using for knees. Before you think that this is the beginning of a tortuous funny story, let me explain that 'knees' are a very important part of a wooden yacht's construction. They are curved pieces of timber, often of oak, which join two pieces of wood which meet at an angle. They have to be very strong and not likely to break across or crack when under strain. Gordon explained that he was to saw his 'knees' out of oak. "Come with me lad," said the old man and hobbled on a stick and an arthritic hip into an empty shed. The floor was covered with leaves and the debris of years of disuse, but the old man's stick began to uncover short branches of trees curved where they had grown naturally from the oak tree from which they had been cut. The grain of these branches followed the curve of branch and would not give under strain. "Here's one, there's another." The old man's stick uncovered knee after knee and at his invitation Gordon filled his car with these prized items. The age old craftsmanship of it appealed so strongly to Gordon's innate sense of what was right.

After months of work, just as the yacht neared completion, Gordon accepted a position as Head of Craft at a new secondary school at Les Quennevais in Jersey. Gordon raced to complete his yacht and eventually launched her and immediately set off for St.Helier on her maiden voyage. Having set off from the Medway, he broke his voyage at Portsmouth where he was joined by Arthur Durner, a 'yard owner from St Aubin in Jersey and Bernard Amy a knowledgeable yachtsman who was to become a close personal friend. Gordon was a born seaman and the navigation was simple for him, but he earnestly wished he had had more time to finish the little craft to his high standards.

I briefly met Gordon one morning in 1965 at Les Quennevais School and we were introduced to each other as fellow yachtsmen. He gave me the immediate impression of a man of great character and depth of feeling. Later on that day I was kneeling in the mud in St.Helier harbour trying against the odds to apply a coat of antifouling to the underwater area of 'Dancing Lady' while the tide was out. But now the tide appeared to be racing across the mud towards me and I realized that I would not be able to finish in time. I became aware of a pair of shoes and the lower part of a pair of trousers standing alongside me. I had no time to chat, but a rich Welsh voice said, "Got another brush boy?" It was Gordon not at all attired for antifouling, but there and then he got stuck in and we finished the job together. That was, as I was to find out over the years, typical of Gordon

His artist's sense of design pervaded everything Gordon touched. His harps and lutes, the sails he measured out on the school hall floor at the weekend, the silver jewellery and trophies showed the measure of the man. So you will understand this moment in time which I am about to relate. By the way, I have not mentioned Gordon's great sense of fun which could send a great burst of laughter from within to remould his face into deep wrinkles of good humour and to set his eyes to flash under those dark eyebrows.

"Here boy, got a moment. Come with me." I was chatting in St.Helier Yacht Club one summer evening when Gordon had appeared at my elbow. I hurried out with Gordon, "I can't tell you. You have to see it for yourself." We hurried to the end of the South Pier. The tide was low. Gordon stopped within ten feet of the pier end and gripping my left arm with his right hand propelled me forward beyond where he now firmly stood with his head turned away back in the direction from which we had just so hurriedly come. He now gestured with an outstretched left arm and hand and fingers flicking my attention to something further on while his right hand now covered his eyes. "It's somewhere down there, I can't bear to look again! It's like a caravan with two broom handles sticking out of its roof."

The 'Compleat Yachtsman'

I immediately saw the cause of Gordon's distress. There squatting on the water some thirty feet below us was the most awful travesty of a yacht. Moulded in fibreglass a tiny galleon complete with miniature "Great Cabin" aft and a low waist with raised forecastle and bowsprit was all set out in something just over twenty feet in length. To Gordon's sensibilities it was a disastrous waste of good materials and time.

Soon Gordon was establishing himself in Jersey as formerly in London, not only as a craftsman, but as a teacher both to adults and to children and was able to convey his tremendous enthusiasm for all crafts to them. Using his time in the craft department at Les Quennevais School he built a small fleet of twelve foot fibreglass dinghies complete with their sails and all their gear. Many boys and girls learned more about craft and the use of tools than in the normal school woodwork and metalwork exercises while working on these little boats. The youngsters then went on to be taught to sail them by Gordon around the nearby St Aubins Bay.

Yvonne too built one of the dinghies for the family while attending Gordon's very popular evening classes where his humour and enthusiasm was appreciated. Gordon soon saw the need for more than just boatbuilding if his students were to use the sea surrounding the Island safely and so he began to teach 'marlinspike' seamanship. That broad approach to things to do with the sea that includes all aspects of boat handling, maintenance and even navigation. It is to the last element of this study that I now refer.

At that time in the late 1960's another Welshman, very different from Gordon Jones was Head of the Evening Classes at Les Quennevais School. More than two thousand Islanders were enrolled for classes ranging across a broad spectrum from Needlework to Car maintenance . Brian Hughes was small in stature, but a fireball of an organizer and very popular with everyone. I had introduced him to sailing aboard 'Dancing Lady' and he soon wanted a small boat in which to potter around the Jersey coast. After some analysis of his requirements we decided that a small inflatable boat capable of carrying four people and with a good quality outboard motor to give about twelve knots was about right . It was trailer mounted and so could be kept at home and taken to any part of the Island. We move back to Gordon.

Gordon had raised the wrath of no less a personage of one Captain 'Bob" Woods R.N. (Ret'd). How had this come about, I

The 'Compleat Yachtsman'

hear you ask. Well 'Bob' was a likable man and was known for his wonderful repartee and long, delightful yarns. But......as an ex naval officer he was very proud of his service career, ex Royal Navy Harbourmaster of Gibraltar, former Commander of the Royal Nigerian fleet of three gunboats etc. He was now teaching Navigation with a capital 'N' in the evening classes and many yachtsmen and professional sailors studied at his knee. He exploded when he heard that Gordon was trespassing into his domain by touching on elementary navigation for his students and he demanded, nay ordered that it should be stopped forthwith.

To settle this row Brian Hughes in his role as Head of the Evening Classes decided that a meeting should be arranged between Gordon and Captain 'Bob'. Brian would also attend, but he wanted me to be chairman. The meeting was without rancour. 'Bob' opened by saying that he knew more about navigation than anyone in the room. True, but hardly the way to encourage a friendly discussion. I gave him that, but pointed out that Gordon was an inspirational teacher of boatbuilding and seamanship and needed to touch on elementary navigation. Soon we had agreement that Gordon would 'do his bit' and leave the deep sea stuff to 'Bob'. What is this diversion all about you say?

Brian Hughes came to see me a month or so later and asked me about taking his inflatable boat to Brittany, towing it there behind his car and using the ferry to St.Malo. I pointed out the French logic in these matters. If you sail into French waters in your boat the French assume that you can handle it safely as you have arrived there. However, if you drive off the ferry........."Excusez-moi m'sieu, but can I see your papers please." Papers that qualify you to safely 'drive' your boat. "I may have something at home," Brian said.

A day or so later he called me over to where he was standing in a quiet corner of the staffroom. He produced a well rubbed, grubby, brown paper envelope of normal letter size and while delving into it a small deckle edged photograph fluttered to the floor. I stooped to pick it up and found myself looking at the deck of a small warship covered in thick ice with sailors chipping and sweeping it off the deck. "Hello Brian, what's this", I asked. "Oh that, that was in the North Atlantic, winter of 1943 I think. We were steaming at two knots head to wind, chipping off ice for fear of capsizing."

At last his stubby fingers produced a creased flimsy of typical services documentation. He put in my hand. "Would the French accept this?" he asked. A Master's Certificate, amended North Atlantic (Winter) was what he had put into my hand. He had sat there quietly, saying nothing while 'Bob' had banged on about his undoubted knowledge of navigation. What reserve, what humility. "Yes Brian, I think that will do nicely," I said.

After that little diversion, to return to Gordon. So many incidents spring to mind; he was always so helpful, giving assistance and advice or the use of his workshop to all his friends. The Chausey Islands lying some twenty miles to the south east of Jersey were as I have already mentioned, a magnet for local sailors. The Hotel run by Madame Blondeau was a source of good food, wine and good company after a race down from Jersey. Gordon was soon initiated into the rites and became a strong competitor in 'Gafr Wen'. On one occasion a tidal miscalculation caused her to lay on her side. Fortunately no damage was done, but with boyish guilt Gordon confessed to me one day after that weekend. His gaze was on the floor and a half smile lit his face as he used his favourite untranslatable

Welsh expression, "Derrrrr" or something like that. "Never mind," I said when he had finally expunged his guilt, "Probably the little White Goat just felt like a nibble of seaweed." Immediately his dark eyebrows shot up into his black unruly hair and he exploded into one of his full throated laughs." "I like it," he crooned and felt that it matched his feelings for his well-loved boat.

Gordon's humour was instant. We were sitting side by side on the raised stage at Les Quennevais School during assembly one morning. The staff lined the front of the stage, while the head sat at a table in the middle. The students, all eight or nine hundred of them, sat in serried ranks on chairs in the hall at a lower level. A member of staff, Colin Hill, the Careers Teacher, was giving forth in his inimitable style about Noah and the construction of the Ark. He had reached that passage from the Bible wherein the dimensions of the Ark to be were handed down by God. I leaned across to Gordon and whispered quietly in his ear, "Narrow gutted bloody thing wasn't it?" If I had known Gordon's reaction I would have held my peace! He exploded with an enormous laugh which nearly took him off his chair and into the body of the students quietly listening to the scriptures. Everyone turned to look at Gordon from the Head downwards while Gordon seized his handkerchief and buried his face in it with great show of recovering from a violent sneezing attack. Typical of Gordon he went immediately after assembly to the Head to apologize.

To return to Chausey……. The summer night was barmy, perhaps sixty yachtsmen and I must not forget, yachtswomen too were enjoying the music flowing from the open hotel windows and doors out into the garden. A three piece band we had 'imported' for the occasion pumped out the pop tunes of the 70's and loud voices and much laughter gave a backcloth to the moonlit Islands and to the distant lights of Normandy and Jersey. Below us in the sound, our yachts strained gently at their anchors in the falling tide. What could be more perfect.

Gordon decided that an improvement could be made. Waving a full litre glass of good French beer and, it must be said, with the assistance of a few more inside him, Gordon indicated, by means of the aforesaid glass, a nearby privet hedge of about four or five feet in height and invited all and sundry to join him in a hedge jumping competition. Encouraged to show his skill in this novel, Welsh sport Gordon was first off and made a good if not entirely successful attempt, handicapped by that glass. His 'flight' ended as his rapidly rotating feet caught the top of the hedge and he nosedived down a steep bank on the other side of that hedge and which he had definitely not calculated on! A broken glass, a cut forehead and a grand black eye was the final result. There was no further competition.

Having sold 'Dancing Lady', Yvonne and I had camped in the New Forest while seeking a replacement yacht on the South Coast. As mentioned elsewhere in this book, we had found the Dutch-built 'Blue Raven', a thirty foot Bermudan sloop. After a small amount of work to ready her for sea, I telephoned Gordon to ask whether he would like to come across and sail her back to Jersey. Gordon readily accepted and was soon with us. His very first reaction was to go across to a nearby pontoon which afforded a good view of 'Blue Raven' looking directly at her port side. "She's a yacht, boy," Gordon purred.

I gave Gordon his head and he enthusiastically double checked everything with me and we set off in the afternoon down the Hamble River for Jersey. In the Channel we had perfect visibility and a fair wind to cross the shipping lanes with the great container ships ploughing across our bows at a remorseless speed. As we approached the Normandy coast to run down the Race with a favourable tide, a mist surrounded us in the early hours. The wind dropped away and we were forced to motor at six knots. Gradually we became aware of the sound of a heavy marine engine off our starboard bow. It came on and we were ready with flares and signals to hand to take evasive action. Our little horn was totally inadequate in the circumstances. GPS and small ship radar were not yet invented.

Then a biggish tug appeared a safe distance off our starboard bow and began to cross our course. Above the wheelhouse coloured lights sent us thumbing through our almanac. It was towing, but what? We watched astern of the tug in the half light and poor visibility. At last a large catamaran hove into view. It was Moitessier's record breaking 'cat', apparently on tow to Cherbourg.

Dawn broke and with it the mist disappeared, but we were not too sure of our position until the French coast happily appeared on the Port bow. I was so tired after the running around to find and then buy 'Blue Raven' and with the long night that I began a mild form of hallucination. Gordon had yielded the tiller to me and I was sure that we were somehow at the end of a long runway and an aircraft was taking off towards our stern. We arrived safely in St.Helier thanks to the help our good friend had given us.

Derek Pritchard was a senior training pilot with British Airways and another close friend of Gordon as well as a partner in a sailing school which they had started. 'Gafr Wen' was to sail up to the South Coast of England the following morning as Gordon chatted with Derek in the Yacht Club. "When are you leaving?" Derek casually asked. "Oh about 3 a.m." "That should be good, just about dawn," rejoined the pilot. At about 07.00 hrs Jersey Airport Control Tower received a radio message from Captain Pritchard who had just taken off for the United Kingdom in a Viscount that there was a small yacht off the North coast of Jersey which seemed to be in difficulties and asking for permission to descend to check up on it. Permission was given.

Gordon had had a good sail up from Jersey so far and 'Gafr Wen' was going well. All quiet, nothing to do but sit at the tiller and chat with his crew or eat a sandwich. Suddenly there was an almighty roar and a four engined, turbo prop' Viscount thundered over his mast at zero altitude, waggled its wings and was gone leaving a shattered Gordon to regain his equilibrium.

Gordon found the time to create some very fine trophies in silver for St.Helier Yacht Club among them a starting canon displayed on an artistic representation of local battlements. Always competitive, he began to position 'Gafr Wen' further up the local fleet by finishing well in Club events some of them long distance. He received a great deal of help and advice from his friend Bernard Amy who was a professional sailmaker and chandler who often crewed with Gordon. 'Gafr Wen's' finest moment came when she placed first on handicap in the 2004 Dresdner Guernsey to Jersey Challenge Race against the strongest competition. It was to be Gordon's swansong as he died shortly afterwards leaving behind him a legacy of craftsmanship, determination and skill threaded through with a strong sense of humour and enjoyment of life.

SEPTEMBER TIDE

If ever there was a dedicated yachtsman, then it must have been the late John Marriner. John was a gentleman; born into the wrong period, his manner and lifestyle belonged to the early twentieth century. His voice too was of that cultured English intonation and marked him as a distinguished person the moment he spoke. He would have fitted seamlessly into the West End social whirl of Noel Coward and that era. His beautiful house 'Les Murailles' was situated overlooking the whole of St Aubin's Bay and was kept in apple pie order by a butler-come-chauffeur and his wife who was a brilliant cook and housekeeper.

I dined with John and a few friends on several occasions and can still recall the perfect reception into his domain. Met by his butler, while your coat was taken in the hall, you were immediately aware of an ambience; a large oil painting of Lieutenant John Marriner. R.N. took you in with timeless gaze and you were swept into an elegant lounge where John might be seated at the grand piano elegantly playing some pieces from a London Musical. "Hello Leo. Help yourself to a drink. Pour me something too, if you please."

He was the perfect host and his guests were always interesting. The Baden-Powells I remember well, on that occasion we started with slivers of raw herring washed down with aquavit served in tiny crystal decanters next to each place setting. John knew everyone and his conversation was elegant and witty drawing out from all his guests the best and most entertaining conversation. He set a standard which few could achieve outside a certain social grouping.

But he had had his 'other' moments too. He regaled us once with his accounts of managing a non-stop, record breaking piano player. It happened in Guernsey in the 1950's, a hall had been hired and the new record breaking attempt was duly advertised throughout the Island. For an admission charge spectators were ushered into the hall and listened while the pianist 'tinkled the ivories'. Of course the non-stop pianist had to play throughout the night and his manager, John, had to be there too. No one came to listen in the 'dog hours' of the night and John and the NSP slept together on top of the piano. You will understand that they could not book a hotel room! Unfortunately they were 'unfrocked' by some wandering insomniac and left Guernsey rather quickly.

It was 'September Tide', a large wooden motor yacht which gave John his entree into the world of yachting. She was a fairly big vessel for the 1960's and unlike many of her sister ships, which are grossly underused, she went long distances and visited many countries. John became a regular and knowledgeable contributor to monthly yachting magazines and wrote articles on several occasions. He also lectured in Yacht Clubs and it was while lecturing at St Helier Yacht Club that I first met him. I was a lowly member of the Entertainment Committee and I was asked to man the slide projector. A billiard cue was used as a pointer and John would tap the butt on the floor to indicate a slide change. He was considered a star attraction and packed the clubs. The audience loved his smooth presentation and unfailing sense of humour.

Immediately after the war it was difficult in England to obtain a new car. Hard currency was badly needed by the British Treasury and all luxury goods were for export only. Now, as a 'war-torn' Island, Jersey was allocated to the Export Area and so luxury items such as a new car became quite readily available. John Marriner ordered a new Vauxhall 'Velox', a car much in the American style, full of chromium plate and with a yawning aperture where more refined cars had an air intake to cool the radiator. The car arrived at Pool's Garage and after it was prepared, the salesman rang John to enquire about delivery. "I will be at South Pier aboard 'September Tide'," John told him. "Please deliver it to me there."

The car was parked on the pier and John came down the gangway of his yacht to take charge of his new toy. Everything settled to his satisfaction, John retired to his yacht, but later on decided to take the car for a spin. He jumped in, started up and selecting first gear on this brand new car drove it straight into a low but substantial granite bollard just out of sight in front of the air intake, which was now somewhat restyled. Amidst the steam from the damaged radiator and other 'sounds off', it is not recorded what the driver said. However, the car was fetched away by a breakdown truck and eventually fully repaired.

"Your car is ready, Sir. Where would you like it to be left?" John was on his yacht again and so some weeks after the incident with the bollard, the car was delivered and inspected to John's entire satisfaction. A little while later he jumped in, started up, selected first gear and drove it into the same bollard as before! John could tell the story to his own discomfort and get pleasure from it. It tells you something about the yachting spirit.

One of his adventures with 'September Tide' was the trip into Eastern Europe, deep behind the Iron Curtain. Unwelcome? Not a bit of it, the English M'Lord charmed the communist hierarchy and he was feted as he navigated the canals and rivers of these then inaccessible countries. More articles ensued and I imagine that he also visited his chums at the Foreign Office in Whitehall to be debriefed.

On one occasion 'September Tide' was sailing across the Adriatic from a port in southern Italy heading for communist controlled Yugoslavia and carefully avoiding the more southerly Albania, which was at that time, an extreme communist state rather like North Korea. If he should land up in Albanian waters, he stood a good chance of being shelled out of the water or captured and imprisoned. Night fell and a tired John made a fatal error. He switched on the autopilot and everyone settled down to sleep. When morning came, it was noticed that the yacht, still under autopilot was sailing round in circles. Big or small circles? The size mattered not, what did matter was for how long? The instrument had jammed to one side when correcting itself and the crucial electric points were welded together. No clue of timespan there.

John decided that the only thing to do as they were now close to the eastern shore of the Adriatic was to head well north and then head in to the coast. He had visas for Yugoslavia, but would this action be enough? Let us suppose that the yacht had not just turned circles, but perhaps had also steered itself well south. The sky was overcast so that a 'fix' was not possible and this was the days before electronic aids. The coast appeared, the yacht sailed on and John was feted once again in communist Yugoslavia.

Eventually 'September Tide' passed on to other owners and John purchased the 'Black Watch' an altogether more imposing steel vessel more like a miniature liner. John loved her and continued his adventures on his newfound toy. He was in many ways 'The Perfect Yachtsman' refined and experienced.

LALUN

Johan Anker, the Norwegian Yacht Designer, laid down the lines for a wonderful new class of sailing yacht during the 1930's. The class was to be called the Dragon. Twenty nine feet in length and with the most beautifully shaped hull they became a classic from the moment of their inception. They were to have a crew of three and to race as a one-design against each other. The class was rapidly taken up internationally and all British Dragons carried a sail number beginning with the identifying letters DK.

DK66 lay in St Peter Port Harbour in the lovely island of Guernsey and she was for sale. Named after a lady of uncertain virtue from a book by Rudyard Kipling, 'Lalun' was the prettiest of yachts. Her hull was dark blue set off with a white waterline and red underwater. Her lines bespoke her speed and manoeuvrability.

Francis bought her from her owner a Mr Fitzgerald for the princely sum of £650 greatly assisted in raising this vast sum by a young lawyer friend, one Vernon Tomes, later to become the Deputy Bailiff of Jersey. I helped somewhat by agreeing to buy 'Redshank' from Francis and everything was set for us to collect

'Lalun'. It was late autumn and the weather was not being very kind to us. Furthermore Francis was restricted, as was I, to sailing on the weekends due to the fact that we were both working. Regardless of the limited weather forecasts available in those days and of the seagoing abilities of a Dragon, Francis and I and a willing friend boarded the mailboat for Guernsey one Friday evening and after a brief visit to the harbour to see 'Lalun' sitting out on an open mooring, we repaired to a nearby hotel.

I rapidly became ill with a high temperature and Francis did everything he could to help me. We were to set off at daybreak and I can scarcely remember the journey to the harbour or the crossing to 'Lalun' in a dinghy. Francis insisted that I went below into the tiny cabin which sported two minimal bunks or slatted wooden benches. I lay down unable to get comfortable while through the little cabin doors my vision was limited to a small patch of grey sky and scudding clouds. I managed to get up to see our 'crew' slip the bow mooring from the buoy and 'Lalun' headed for the harbour entrance.

The movement of the hull was firm and positive and felt so much more seaworthy than our Falcon. Occasionally the crest of a large wave hove into view through my framed vision and the yacht vibrated with speed and I could hear the rapid passage of water along the hull beside my ear. With a strong westerly wind Lalun was reaching along at maximum hull speed and making an excellent passage time to Jersey. In close on four hours we covered the distance from Guernsey to Jersey, some thirty miles and were mightily impressed with the Dragon. Little did I realise just how dangerous a Dragon could be driving into a heavy sea, but I reached home and fell into bed with a bad bout of flu.

Francis now began to trick out 'Lalun' with cruising equipment. Melamine mugs and plates were placed aboard, knives and cutlery followed. A gimballed primus stove was found which had come off Westward, T.B. Davis' 'J' class yacht and we began to cruise.

Francis' first venture was to Sark. It was a lovely day and 'Lalun' sailed to perfection. If you have never sailed a Dragon I can only say that everything you would expect a good yacht to do the Dragon did to perfection. It tacked immediately and sailed so close to the wind with just the smallest flicker of the jib near the masthead to hint that you might just be a little too close.

Sark hove into view and we sailed into the tiny Le Creux harbour for the night. Accommodation was limited and we had four on board, so that I found myself a berth in the cockpit under a canvas cover stretched over the boom, shared with another crew member. Yvonne was more fortunate and was allocated a berth below. Morning broke and we could not wait to get to sea again. The wind was light and a slight seamist came up as the little wind there was fell away. A trusty Seagull outboard motor with a strange hull side mounting on the starboard quarter was deployed and ran quite sweetly pushing us on course for Grosnez Point.

Grosnez Point has a profile rather like a giant face or head, hence the 'gros nez' or big nose. Coming out of the fog on course to Jersey one day many years ago, an old Southern Railways steamer, I believe it was the 'Autocarrier', came upon Grosnez Point at quite close quarters and had to go astern very quickly. We too saw it quite close and turned away now sure of our position while Francis, our master navigator plied his trade.

Then after a while the Seagull became sick and stopped. Plug changes and other coaxing eventually saw it cough into life again and run unhappily, but we made our moorings in St Helier Harbour. A close examination of the little motor when it was taken ashore revealed that all the water cooling passageways in the motor were choked with hardened salt evaporated from the seawater by the heat of the engine. The engine had been running too hot. The simple cure was to fasten it onto the edge of a fifty gallon drum of freshwater and to leave it running until all the salt had dissolved away.

Francis was not interested in local buoy hopping events and wanted to test 'Lalun's' mettle against the larger cruising yachts against whom he felt she would perform well. However, wiser voices prevailed and much to Francis' disappointment the Sailing Committee refused to accept his request to compete in the 'cruising class' events. No amount of persuasion would shift their position. Francis was determined and fought on. At last it was agreed that if he fitted 'Lalun' with a self draining cockpit, the Sailing Committee would reconsider.

Now Dragons were really an open boat in which the cockpit was just slatted wooden seats fastened to the bare hull and although there was a short cabin, any wave coming aboard in rough weather would have entered every part of the hull causing problems. One could see the Sailing Committee's point. To install a self draining cockpit would have been a major undertaking, costly and adding greatly to the weight of the yacht. Francis declined the offer.

I read later the account of a Dragon which when cruising off the east coast of England ran into steep seas and began to run her

Illustration by
Peter Richards

long narrow bow deep into them until she was swamped. The crew was lucky to be picked up. Francis was unaware of this and, as you will learn, so was I. Francis decided to prove 'Lalun' against the cruisers by accompanying them part of the way on their coming race to St Malo.

Gillian was Francis girlfriend at the time and competent crew and as I was not available Francis and Gillian were aboard the Dragon as she was sailing among the early morning cruisers on the starting line. Careful not to impede the yachts entered for the race, Francis set off well for the north Minquiers buoy, the first mark of the course, fully intending to turn back when he reached it. 'Lalun' sailed well and kept up with the leaders, but when the mark was reached Francis found it difficult to give up and turn round and so our intrepid pair found themselves that very afternoon in St Malo.

The other crews were quite impressed by the Dragon's performance and made sure that Francis and Gillian would come along to their dinner that evening at the St Malo Yacht Club. Francis and Gillian, short of cash as they did not intend this 'visit', searched to borrow a dress for Gillian and eventually a kind stewardess at the club obliged. It now became clear that rather than persuading the Sailing Committee to allow the Dragon to compete in future offshore events, the Committee were now more firmly resolved not to allow her in.

Added to their concerns about seaworthiness, now they saw that the lightly equipped 'Lalun' would have unfair advantage over the heavily built cruising yachts which would be difficult to allow for under the handicap measurements. This was to be

Francis' first and last 'cruising event'. His pluck and determination was admired, but "No," was the answer to his request.

Shortly after this Francis was commissioned into the Royal Air Force and while serving at R.A.F. Thorney Island on the south coast, he joined the Royal Air Force Sailing Association. He then sailed in various offshore races including the Fastnet aboard 'Jethou' the sister ship of the well-known Jersey yacht 'Tien-Ho', and he also sailed in the very successful 'Dambuster'. Meanwhile, I now found myself in ownership of a fine Dragon.

Cruising events were far from my mind and with two or three good deepkeel yachts to compete against, I was soon racing round the buoys in St Aubin's Bay. 'Lalun' was perfect and so responsive.

Tony Messiter was the former R.A.F fighter pilot who had introduced me to pottering offshore in 'Ariel', his little Edwardian sloop. Now Tony joined the crew of 'Lalun' along with Ken Parry also formerly of the R.A.F and a Welshman hailing from Angelsey. I particularly recall the Troy Trophy race from St Helier to Gorey when sailing well against Ronnie Taylor's 'Swallow', we came down onto the Conchiere, a large rock off the south east coast of Jersey and a mark of the course. Ronnie decided to indulge in a tacking duel with me right on top of the Conchiere which was well covered with water, but around which the sea swirled and rose and fell.

A large granite rock close to, even if sunlit, is quite an impressive sight. George Hairon, a local fisherman and a good friend to the members of St Helier Yacht Club was stationed as the mark boat just off the ominous rock and he yelled at us, "Get off, you're over the Conchiere," but Ronnie would not yield nor would I. At last, I managed to break free from Ronnie and with a fresh breeze tore towards the distant finish line at Gorey pierhead. The gun was fired for us as we streamed across the finishing line. We had won our class. The wad which holds the powder firmly into the blank cartridge of a twelve bore signal gun sometimes catches fire and is propelled a good distance beyond the smoke of the gun. In an identical position just below the gun at Gorey pierhead, Bill Morvan had the wad pass through his jib and Bill had quipped to the Committee members above, "You fired that gun late!" For the shot should have gone ahead of the forestay.

Bob Kempster now came sailing with me and naturally took the helm. He brought with him Alfie Cartwright then a young lad. I learned a great deal from both and was very happy to let them handle 'Lalun'. Gorey Regatta was coming up soon and it was unfortunate that work prevented me from competing in some of the races for the deepkeel yachts. So when Bob offered to compete with her on my behalf I was very pleased and readily agreed. Bob phoned me in the late afternoon when I was at home to give me an account of the day's sailing and also to inform me of an incident in which he had collided with a racing dinghy. Bob knew little about the racing rules, but was sure that I would hear from the dinghy's owner, a young lawyer, Peter Crill, later to be Sir Peter Crill and Bailiff of Jersey. I asked Bob to tell me exactly what had happened.

It seems that two separate races were being run off at the same time and shared one mark of the course. 'Lalun' was coming down fast onto this mark while sailing with the wind coming over her starboard bow. Approaching fast from starboard and on the port tack came a planing dinghy, a 505, one of the large racing dinghies then well fancied by the racing man. The helmsman of the 505 attempted to pass ahead of Bob, calling for 'water' as he did so intent on, rounding the mark ahead of 'Lalun'. He had misjudged it badly and 'Lalun' had sailed right over the Jollyboat, which did not improve its varnish work.

Sure enough the phone rang later that evening, but not before I had scanned the racing rules. It was Peter. To whom should he direct the account for the repair of his 505, now in the yard awaiting repair. It is difficult for a young chap who is not trained in legal matters to explain to one of Jersey's cleverest lawyers that he may have got it wrong. I admit to being nervous while I explained to him that since Bob was on the starboard tack, the right of way tack, giving him precedence at the mark, that he was in the wrong! After an explosion of legal eloquence at the other end of the phone, Peter graciously accepted that he was at fault. Fortunately there was little or no damage to the Dragon. It is as well to leave some things alone.

So to continue the Gorey race, we took the gun and immediately with some jubilation sailed on to find the orange buoy of a mooring I had borrowed which lay somewhere among the lines of yachts. Ken was up on the foredeck holding a light anchor with line attached and I called out to him that the anchor would not be needed but he was new to sailing and did not realise that the buoy would be fastened to permanent mooring chains. I spotted the buoy off to starboard and pointing it out to

Lalun

Ken and Tony put the helm down to turn onto it. To my astonishment there was an almighty splash and Ken and the anchor disappeared into the water as he jumped overboard to secure the mooring. 'Lalun' came up all standing as Ken and the anchor together bit the sand! I had never seen such selfless devotion to a yacht before. We could not gather later from a contrite Ken exactly what he thought he was doing.

Jo was Ken's beautiful wife, but she not only looked very lovely, she also had one of the most caring attitudes to life I have ever come across. Just to illustrate this point, may I recount one small incident. Ken was Head of Music at St Helier Boys School and lived in a small cottage just at the entrance to the school's driveway. One of the staff of the school was a well-known character, a bachelor and unlike many of his persuasion, rather neglectful of his personal appearance and dare I say hygiene. Many of us smiled at this poor man's condition and to our shame, did nothing to help him. When Jo came from Wales with Ken to their new post she very soon made many friends and among them took our bachelor under her wing. In no time she had shown such a close personal and caring interest in him that he sported a colourful scarf knitted by Jo and all his clothing was washed or dry cleaned, care of Jo. What a transformation.

Ken and Jo began sailing with Yvonne and me and we enjoyed little 'trips around the bay'. One evening, when everything had been arranged to go out in 'Lalun', Ken phoned to say that something had come up and he could not go out with us but that Jo would love to go rather than stay at home. So Yvonne, Jo and I sailed out of the harbour on a lovely summer evening in a light breeze. After perhaps three hours of enjoyable sailing we turned from within the bay towards the harbour and the breeze promptly died. There was not a breath of wind to fill the sails. The trusty Seagull outboard motor was at home, as I never carried it when set up for racing. However, there was a very long pair of oars or 'sweeps' aboard the Dragon, part of her original equipment and although she could be rowed with them, as she was fitted with rowlocks, I chose to scull her back to her mooring.

It was a slow progress towards the harbour and darkness fell. I was totally unprepared for sailing at night and as we entered the pierheads at St Helier, the watchman was surprised and came out to advise me of the need for lights! Ken was waiting anxiously on the landtie, but Jo and Yvonne were so happy with our little adventure. Sadly, after Jo and Ken left Jersey for a new post in the south of England, Jo was killed in a car accident.

The Dragon's days were numbered. On a Bank Holiday weekend, I took Yvonne to Chausey, a French group of islands some twenty miles to the south east of Jersey. We intended to stay overnight, Yvonne in a little borrowed tent and me aboard in the spartan accommodation of 'Lalun'. We sailed down in beautiful weather with a fine quartering breeze, 'Lalun' bowling along at six knots. Entering by the north passage to the sound of Chausey, we met up with Dudley Harrison coming out on his way home in 'Taquah' a 1900's converted fishing craft. She made a fine sight as with full gaff rig she ploughed out towards us. We converged our courses as Dudley was a good friend and called out to each other, Dudley had been fishing and as we passed close by he threw over two mackerel for our lunch.

We moored up in our favourite bay, just below a little chapel and shipping our drying legs soon rested on the beach and we were able to walk ashore. The following day was Saturday and we spent it roaming the island, swimming and enjoying Madame Blondeau's Hotel. For those who do not know Chausey, it is a wonderful archipelago of little islands. The main island, graced by a large granite lighthouse which is such a feature of the nightlife as it blazes out its signal, has no roads and is in some ways rather like Sark. The Renault family of car manufacturing fame reconstructed a chateau there at the turn of the century and used to arrive from Paris in an enormous electric launch which was kept at the nearby port of Granville only a few miles away. The launch had its own slipway at Chausey and came up out of the water on a light railway drawn by a powerful winch installed in a large hangar. Now the whole affair is still very complete, but in disuse.

That night, the Saturday, a huge wind arrived. It blew so strongly that I had to use my inflatable dinghy to set two additional moorings to restrain 'Lalun' in quite a wild sea. Fortunately we were within the bay and sheltered from the worst of the wind. But the wind was not my greatest worry, it was the lightning. I was aboard a yacht with a tall mast rising above much of the surrounding rocks and structures and the steel rigging came right through the deck and terminated on internal chainplates at my feet. By morning the wind had abated somewhat and Yvonne arrived aboard after quite an exciting night holding her tent down in an impossible wind, a plucky girl.

Totally lacking experience of cruising and sea conditions, I decided that the Sunday morning was just the time to sail back to Jersey! Conditions within the islands were quite good and the thunderstorm had long since passed over. We cleared the north passage and turned for home. Straight away I found the sea state was at the limit of what the Dragon could cope with. The high winds overnight had kicked up a big sea and the strong breeze, now we were in the open sea, made our small and finely drawn yacht plunge and lift at great speeds among breaking crests all round us.

It was brought home to me very quickly that the long nose of 'Lalun' would at any moment drive through a wave and we would be in serious trouble as water filled the open cockpit. Keeping as direct a course for Jersey by compass as the conditions would allow, I prayed and steered a line down each wave into its deep hollow then pulled the tiller over and allowed the hull to climb the approaching wave at an angle thus keeping the sharp bow out of the direct line of trouble. It worked. I could see that Yvonne was very frightened and I tied her in with a rope around her waist. We had very little lifesaving equipment aboard in those days. Most of the modern gear we have now had not been invented. Apart from bulky Kapok filled lifejackets all we had was one or two flares and a very small inflatable dinghy tied across the after deck and threatening to break loose as water rushed around it. Radios were heavy items in those days and required substantial batteries so we had none.

I should have reefed to reduce sail before leaving the bay in Chausey, but this sensible precaution was beyond my limited knowledge gathered in sailing close inshore around Jersey. Now reefing was impossible. The deck was awash, there were no guardrails and it was asking too much of Yvonne to hold the tiller in these conditions. We creamed on at high speed spilling as much wind as possible, but it seemed that we must be doing eight or ten knots. Very enjoyable on another day, but now! Now we would be overjoyed just to see the Demie des Pas tower and St Helier behind it. At last we did. In perhaps three hours we had raced across from Chausey to St Helier. A huge continuous swell now began to lift us as we approached the south coast and we accelerated to surfing speeds down its face only to slow right down as the next hill of water approached us, but at last we found ourselves racing past the Elizabeth Castle breakwater and soon entering the friendly pierheads.

Yvonne could not wait to get off 'Lalun and I put her alongside the granite steps on the Albert pier where shivering with fright or cold she made her way up to terra firma in her little yellow oilskins. I knew she would never cruise in 'Lalun' again.

Marshal Doran was a Canadian of Irish stock. Tall and well built with a warm voice and friendly nature. He greatly admired the Dragon and had sailed in her on one occasion. "If ever you want to sell her," he had said, "give me the chance to buy her." Now he said, "Let's play haggles for 'Lalun'. Come to dinner at the restaurant." Marshal ran Doran's a fine hotel and restaurant in St Helier and one evening soon after I sat happily beside Yvonne while Marshal and his charming wife royally entertained us. The price was agreed at £750, a full hundred pounds more than I had paid for her and although I was sad to see her go, I knew that she was going to a good home. Yvonne and I now had our hearts set on a cruising yacht.

CHAUSEY

Chausey, was one of our haunts where we often sailed into a lovely little bay and settled down onto the beach just below a little old chapel. Bliss! In those days the islands had only a few local residents, mostly the families of fishermen who used small open sailing boats with loose-footed gaff sails. They sometimes had a regatta and a blessing of the fleet.

Marin Marie, the famous French single-handed sailor also lived there in a lovely house with extensive views over the islands. He was a gifted artist too and had crossed the Atlantic three times alone in the 1930's. His 'Ariel' a fine, tough motorboat of about forty feet lay nearby on the beach. He had made a 16mm, black and white film of his crossing in 'Ariel' and there is in it a thrilling moment when off the Nantucket Light, with his steering locked up into an old fashioned self steering system, he came too close to the liner 'La France' doing thirty knots. He had arranged for 'Ariel' to be filmed by a friend from the liner's deck and so set a course to close the great ship. Marin Marie then went on deck to film the 'La France" I believe it was, with a 16 mm cine camera. He filmed away and when he took the viewfinder from his eye, there was the huge vessel almost right on top of 'Ariel'! Just a matter of camera viewfinders making things look further away than they really are!

Chausey

To wander around the traffic free island in the fresh air and sunshine with your little white yacht nestling in a bay just nearby was idyllic. We often went up to the Renault family chateau on the island. It was an imposing granite building which seemed to fit quite nicely into its surroundings. It had been a ruin when bought by the Renaults who had rebuilt it as a country retreat. They used to come down from their home in Paris in a huge Renault touring car, arriving at the port of Granville just across from Chausey they would board a one hundred foot electric launch and sail silently to the island. After they had disembarked, the launch would glide around to a purpose built slipway and settling onto a rail carriage would be drawn up a light railway and into a huge shed for maintenance. The shed still stood, but the Renaults were no longer there. Inside the shed all sorts of souvenirs of their time were to be seen. Renault advertising plaques and some tools and benches, but the railway had rusted away.

Madame Blondeau ran a small hotel and restaurant on the island, I cannot recall the name of the hotel, because we always called it Madame Blondeau's. It was the scene of many unforgettable visits. St.Helier Yacht Club sometimes ran races to the island and one was for the Blondeau Cup. Madame was a delightful person who always made the visiting yachtsmen at home and even gave every race entrant a prize. Our first event in 'Dancing Lady' saw us motoring in to the moorings in light winds so we did not even finish the race, but Madame gave us a lovely fish made of animal horn which we still have.

However, the most memorable night was when the club sailed down for a rally to Chausey and we brought down our own piano, no not a grand piano, but a full size upright aboard a Jerscy fishing boat. The dinner and celebrations went on into the early hours and I distinctly recall looking back from the wet beach to Madame Blondeau's set high on the island. The music swept over us and the lights from the hotel danced on the wet sand and so did the hotel!

The following morning, afloat in the sound I was awakened by distant shouts and poked my head out of the hatch to see what was going on. Someone had been to each yacht in the small hours of the morning and had rounded up all our dinghies and tied them up on a buoy well into the middle of the sound and out of reach of any anchored yacht. It transpired that on the previous night, a reveller had climbed up the mast of Graham Godfray's yacht and had tied at the masthead a large wooden pig holding a menu usually situated outside Madame Blondeau's. With great thought he had then hauled up all the halliards to the top of the mast and had fastened them off. Shinning down he had made his escape. The air was blue as Graham's attention was drawn by nearby crews to his new masthead pennant. Now we were all being rewarded by Graham for enjoying his earlier predicament. There was nothing for it but to swim for your dinghy, which we did.

Graham Godfray was a very capable yachtsman often doing well in club races. I was with Dudley Harrison aboard his gaff cutter 'Taquah' and we were lying for the weekend in Chausey Sound. We had come in by way of the south entrance which was a very straightforward piece of navigation. However, there was another entrance to Chausey Sound which came in from the north through a complicated passage surrounded by rocks and islands. This entrance could only be attempted an hour or so each side of high water and the navigation of it depended on lining up various marks, sometimes a large Tower, the Enseigne, with the island's lighthouse, but other marks were not so obvious. A pile of cemented stone blocks painted white lining up with a similar heap further back and so on.

The north entrance was much quicker and lay directly on a course set from Jersey. We used to love our navigation in those days. We only had charts and a variety of navigational tools such as dividers and tricky little gadgets often bought from ex government supply stores. Tidetables and Admiralty Tidal Charts also played their part as we navigated at five knots. You can understand why a new and quicker entrance to a favourite group of islands held some attraction for us.

Graham knew the north entrance and used it so Dudley, over a beer in Madame Blondeau's on the Saturday evening asked Graham if we could follow him out in the morning when he left for Jersey. It was all agreed and on Sunday morning both yachts set off together heading for the surrounding reef and the entrance. Graham led in his gaff cutter 'Onyx', one of the oldest yachts still in use and built as an open fishing craft in the 1800's. 'Taquah' followed, both under motor because of the twists and turns of this entrance. All went well at first, Graham kept calling out and pointing to the various marks so that we would see and remember them. All of a sudden we found ourselves following 'Onyx' round in a tight circle, round and round we went as Dudley held 'Taquahs' small wheel hard over. Just as we began to think that something was far from right, Graham turned around and laughed. He knew that we could not escape and was having a bit of fun at our expense! Soon we reached the open sea and having noted the marks nearly always came into Chausey by the North Passage.

There were several other passages around Chausey and some French yachtsman of an artistic bent had drawn them out on a chart which hung framed in Madame's bar. It was entitled the Metro de Chausey after the Paris underground. It was from Chausey that the Baron de Rouillecourt made his final move on the south east coast of Jersey when he attempted to take the island in 1781. Historic and beautiful the islands were a yachtsman's dream in those days. Now just a little too much visited by trippers from nearby Granville and a little too restricted. Where we used to wander freely now wired off, but still very lovely.

Granite of an unusual clean grey colour was quarried in Chausey and some was used in Jersey. I believe that St Thomas' Church in Val Plaisant is built of it. The granite rocks around could tell many tales of shipwreck. One incident I well recall was when a yacht builder, newly started in the business and sailing single-handed, Came down on the north side of Chausey at night. I understand that he was doing sea trials of his new fibreglass prototype yacht of about twenty-six feet overall. He encountered one of the outlying rocks and stuck fast. Seeing the nearby lighthouse swinging its big beam he decided to release a flare or two to summon help. No doubt a little panic stricken, he fumbled in his cockpit locker to find the cardboard box of flares he had loaded aboard among all the other paraphernalia surrounding it. At last he dragged the appropriate box out and dumping it on the cockpit seat with the yacht at a crazy angle struggled to get it open. The sea lifted and dropped the stern with sickening crunching and scraping noises as the cardboard flaps

Chausey

at last opened up. A flare was grabbed, too dark to see the instructions so clear to read in the calm of a harbour or even on the manufacturer's stand at the Boatshow. Here was the trigger thing at the top, hold it steady, point it up to the dark sky and twist the lever. Unfortunately, clearly stated on the invisible instructions you were warned that the trigger was at the bottom of the flare and that the other end should point to the sky. Bang and a parachute flare was fired directly into the open box containing several other flares.

Attracted by the large display of coloured light the Chausey fishermen manned a boat and found the yacht burning well with the builder clinging to the bow. They hauled him aboard frightened, but unhurt and then bucketed water over the fire and salvaged what was left of the yacht on the rising tide.

Sailing small boats is a great education, there are so many things to learn and you will never learn them all. Perhaps the first and most important lesson is this. The open sea is a desert and when you are on it you are relying on your own resources, there will be little or no immediate help or anyone to turn to. So, prepare well and think ahead.

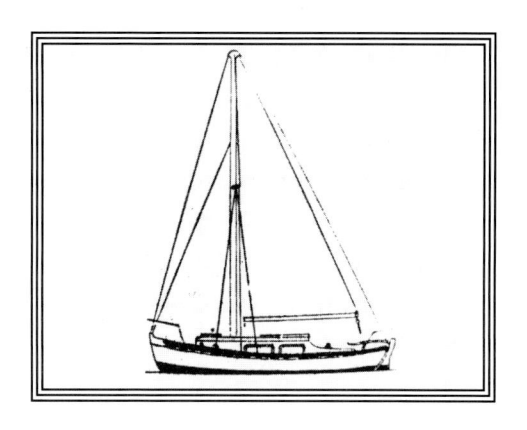

DANCING LADY

St Jean Birt was a leading surgeon. A handsome and charming man, he was idolised by the nurses at the General Hospital. Many a little heart beat faster under its strict uniform when Mr Birt came nearby. Yvonne was no less affected. I had never met Mr Birt, but knew him by sight and had often seen his fine yacht, 'Dancing Lady' sailing off the Island crewed by the joint owners St Jean Birt and Hamish Mitchell, a farmer from the east of the Island.

'Dancing Lady' was built in 1926 by James McGruer, a Scottish yacht builder, long established and with a reputation for building fine little ships. She was built for display on the McGruer stand at the Scottish Exhibition in Glasgow and was purchased by her then first surgeon. Gaff rigged and sporting a bowsprit, she was of carvel construction and had the typical McGruer canoe stern. She had come to Jersey under the ownership of a certain Mr Husband who was given to altering yachts and even building one or two as a hobby. Husband decided that 'Dancing Lady' should be a bermudan rig and that she should also have a much bigger cabin. Away went the cheeky bowsprit and the well balanced rig calculated by a first class designer, David McGruer and in its place went a poorly calculated triangular mainsail and an ugly cabin studded with eight large brass portholes. How to spoil a perfect yacht in no time at all.

There she stood dried out on the beach in tidal St Aubin's Harbour. Yvonne and I recognized immediately that she was right for us in many ways. At twenty-seven feet in overall length and with a long lead keel on which to dry out, she also had a new Commodore diesel engine. Arthur Durner, like so many of the seagoing fraternity, was a real character. A man of few words and strong opinions, it was his sign aboard 'Dancing Lady' that said she was for sale. We made our way to his sail loft and office on the waterfront of the pretty little harbour and found Arthur 'at home'. "Oh yes, she's for sale alright, her owners have ordered a new yacht. She's got a new motor in her too, so their asking £1500 for her".

£1500 was more than I cared to stretch to at that time, so I thanked Arthur and left. Later at South Pier I was talking to Gerald Baudains, the shipyard manager about my interest in 'Dancing Lady'. Gerald was yet another character. Intelligent and with a gift for the control and organisation of 'his' 'yard. The 'yard was spotless and every item of equipment was painted light blue or yellow and had its appointed place. Ladders, shovels, ropes, wedges and many, many other items of a nautical origin, all arraigned in serried ranks around his airy domain. I have seen many other 'yards, but none came near to Gerald's in its perfection.

His voice was deep and carried clearly. "How much would you pay for her?" he asked. I looked at Yvonne, she was as surprised as I was. We had only mentioned 'Dancing Lady' in passing and had intended to ask Gerald if he knew of a small cruising yacht more suited to my not very deep pocket. I told Gerald that £1000 was about my limit for in the 1960's you could have bought close on three new cars for that price. "Leave it with me," Gerald said. "I'll see what I can do?" The phone call at home was unexpected. It was Gerald. "I've spoken to St Jean Birt. How would £1100 do?" We could not believe our good fortune and agreed at once to meet with Mr Birt and his partner aboard 'Dancing Lady' at Gorey Harbour.

Tall and distinguished with unruly white hair St Jean at once displayed his best quality, a mischievous sense of humour. With Yvonne and I seated in the main cabin together with Hamish, St Jean assumed his 'throne' with typical medical humour. It was the yacht's toilet which faced aft down the centre of the hull and was curtained off when 'in use'. Yvonne could scarcely contain her excitement. To be with her hero and to be discussing the purchase of 'Dancing Lady', well, it was almost too much for a girl!

St Jean, in his element, regaled us with stories about their adventures while Hamish of a more reserved Scottish nature contributed now and then. "Did you ever hear of our shark fishing?" demanded St Jean, eyes a twinkle. It seems, as we soon heard, that when they had first purchased her, they had decided to go looking and fishing for a shark. With what they called their 'rubby dubby bag', a sack of fresh offal dropped over the side somewhere to the west of the Island and a long, strong line and large hook well-baited with meat they waited. Suddenly the line ran out fast and when it was restrained had a great weight on it. They had a shark!

Now remember that 'Dancing Lady' was twenty-seven feet long and being a sailing boat, she had rigging coming off the mast and fastened to the hull, bow, stern and each side by chainplates. The shark now began to circle the yacht and St Jean found himself 'dancing' around the deck of his aptly named yacht passing the line quickly around each new obstruction and soon, some he had seen before!

At last the shark was hauled aboard into the small cockpit by the efforts of both our noble fishermen where it lay across the coaming exhausted. Viewed from the cabin top, the only safe vantage point, for it was a pretty big shark. There was no place from which to man the cockpit while it lay there. Suddenly the shark exploded into life and began to leap violently in the stern of the boat. A powerful shark of this size could in its last throes demolish the lightly built cockpit and even bring down the all important backstay. Our heroes now regretted their initial enthusiasm to catch a shark and assisted by the willing fish managed to get it overboard, but only after a very long struggle. That was the end of their careers as shark fishermen.

Yvonne and I were enthralled by the boat and her owners and we immediately agreed to buy her. It seemed weeks had passed before all the formalities of purchasing a Lloyd's Registered yacht had been completed, but at last she was ours. We set too with a will to bring her up to scratch and at last, newly painted and including a change of colour for her bottom from red to blue we took her off her St Helier Harbour mooring and hoisting sail began to sail her across the harbour not far away from a large and very new yacht. It was St Jean and Hamish in their new yacht 'Chanterelle'. 'Dancing Lady' was well heeled and showing off her new blue colour when with Yvonne and I sitting up on the edge of the cockpit St Jean called over, "Very tiddly, we like her bottom." But Yvonne, from working as a nurse with a top surgeon, knew which 'bottom' he was referring to!

So began a long and happy relationship with our new and treasured possession. As with all young ladies, although she was good looking she soon revealed one or two problems. Firstly she would not 'come about' under sail. That is to say she would not tack through the wind but would stall when nearly head to wind and fall away back on her original tack. It took a burst of engine power to get her round. The second problem was that she would not take full power from her very large 2.2 litre diesel engine, but dug her stern lower and lower into the sea until her after deck was awash. Not a pretty sight.

I decided to consult the builders, James McGruer, on the Clyde in Scotland. I had an immediate reply to my letter outlining my problems in which I had also praised the quality and detail of 'Dancing Ladys' construction. The letter was not from James McGruer, but from his father David, an elderly gentleman living in retirement. It was a delightful, long letter and enclosed with it was a blue print of our yacht as she was originally built and rigged as a gaff cutter with a bowsprit. David explained that she had been built for the Scottish Exhibition in 1926 and had been purchased by a surgeon who had kept her on a lake. He went on to describe the build up of her hollow mast and how her full length pitch pine timbers were cut in a special way at the saw mill in the same fashion as that used by the Norsemen. It was a most interesting description of a yacht's construction and it was obvious that David had strong feelings for her even after all the years had passed since she was built in his 'yard.

His most important suggestion was to rig her again as a gaff cutter, which I should have done, but the cost would have been high and she would have been more complicated to handle than her Bermudan rig. He also suggested an improvement to the rudder by extending it aft at its lower end. This was done and greatly improved her handling, she now 'came about' quite well although she had to be moving well through the water before she responded.

Racing in club events or cruising, 'Dancing Lady' now gave us great enjoyment and Yvonne, now Mrs Yvonne Harris, added to our crew. Alison at a few months old occupied one of the main bunks down below in her cane basket and was never a moments bother, in fact we believe that she enjoyed the movement of the yacht. There is nothing quite like having a family aboard a cruising yacht. It changes your perspective completely. The sea conditions are more closely watched and various new considerations affect the equipment carried such as pushchairs and potties! But when our younger daughter Frances joined us it was an additional pleasure, although a lot more work for Yvonne.

Through my work as a teacher I was in close touch with teenagers and often asked the older girls to babysit for us. They were wonderful. Then the idea came to me to see if one would accompany us for a little cruise. Jean Tozer was the first to volunteer and came with us on a three week trip to Brittany, which was a great success. Yvonne was able to share the two children with her and Jean loved the new experience of sailing.

Dancing Lady

Later on Diana Le Bot came aboard and she too soon settled in for other cruises.

One day in 1968 I was down on the beach beside 'Dancing Lady' where she had dried out when I noticed a dark patch on her curved stern post which being a canoe stern, gathered all the planks of the hull together at this point. I examined it and taking my car ignition key out of my pocket poked the patch with it. It sank effortlessly into rotten wood.

I will not bore you with all the details, but many months later I had replaced the complicated elm stern post with a seasoned oak one. In December that year I wrote a lengthy article for 'Yachting Monthly'. It was, I suppose, my first venture into writing. The editor, JD Sleightholme was a very amusing man and later came to Jersey to give a talk at St Helier Yacht Club. Tall and languid he relaxed completely and kept his audience interested and very amused.

I particularly remember his tale of 'Hoshi', the Islands Sailing School's schooner of substantial size.

She was leaving Cherbourg one night and had to motor for lack of wind into a heavy swell which caused her to roll. She had aboard a party who had chartered her for a weekend trip and she was skippered by Sleightholme. There was a long flight of steps in a companionway leading down to the saloon and halfway down this flight was a small landing giving off into the ship's heads (loo) on the starboard side.. As Sleightholme made his way down the steps the yacht rolled heavily to port and a lady burst out of the toilet door to his right and kangaroo hopped across the landing restrained around her ankles by a certain item of underwear. She slammed into the bulkhead to the left of the landing. 'Hoshi' then played her trump card and rolled immediately to starboard causing the lady to stagger backward into her original position and the door to slam behind her.

Our skipper wondered whether he had just seen that or not, it happened so quickly and was such a surprise. Neither party mentioned the incident.

Back to 'Dancing Lady'. After many pleasant adventures, the time came when we could afford a younger and perhaps better yacht more capable of competing in racing.

GRANVILLE

We were sailing to Granville from St Helier on the perfect summer's day, the sun shone down and the breeze came from the west. We bowled along with a full genoa. Perhaps two miles away to the south a white yacht, bigger than ourselves came through the Chausey reef on a passage we did not know, one of the 'Metro' lines we had never used, and glided along under a neat cruising spinnaker on the same course. It was 'Fleur des Iles' the steel Brabant class yacht of Fred Langlois. She was nicely handled by David Fred's son and gybed and turned as she came through the passage, a pleasure to watch.

Clear of the reef, in the open sea she tossed and gently plunged like a young pony, in no hurry to reach Granville. In those days the port of Granville had no marina and visiting yachts had to arrive an hour or so before or after high water when the inner harbour gate stood open. There was no lock so the enormous gate held back sufficient water when shut to keep all the yachts and fishing boats afloat while beyond it the tide receded until the tall harbour walls stood gaunt above the drying beach.

Both yachts arrived at the approaches to the harbour, 'Dancing Lady' well behind 'Fleur'. We dropped our sails preparatory to entering and started our engine, but to our surprise 'Fleur' headed straight for the entrance still under sail and still carrying her spinnaker. It was going to be a neat bit of seamanship to enter with a full spinnaker still set. 'Fleur' had all of our attention as at a good six knots she creamed towards the tricky entrance. She had to sail parallel to the outer harbour wall then turn to port to enter the outer harbour and within a few yards turn sharply to starboard to pass through the gate and drop her spinnaker and mainsail. Some trick, some skill. We waited and watched.

Wind can behave very oddly and often quite logically. The breeze filling that spinnaker was the same breeze that carried past 'Fleur' to hit the tall harbour wall and to be deflected at an acute angle so that as soon as the spinnaker entered the tricky zone it suddenly and to the great surprise of 'Fleur's' crew, filled at right angles to the desired course and the breeze piped up to become a good deal fresher. The helmsman found himself with the tiller now hauled up under his chin to starboard as his gallant little yacht heeled heavily to starboard and taking the bit between her teeth accelerated nicely ignoring his urgent request to turn to port and instead headed quickly straight for the tall granite harbour wall right ahead.

There could be no saving 'Fleur', We froze with anticipation as we watched the accident develop. It was too late for the crew to follow her round parallel to the wall and the helmsman was now struggling to gather himself up from the corner of the cockpit where the sudden heeling of the yacht had landed him still clutching the tiller with white knuckles and still imploring her to turn to port. We knew there would be the most awful scrunching of steel against granite and the crack of breaking timber as the mast came down forward over the bow. Just in the nick of time there was a loud 'crack' which echoed off the harbour walls and the white spinnaker exploded into many pieces and floated oh so gently away on the breeze to starboard. 'Fleur' now relieved of the embarrassment of her spinnaker shot bolt upright and with full port helm on, held there by a skipper frozen with horror, bolted to port with a toss of her head and then, turning immediately to starboard, swept past the open gate and into the inner harbour carrying the remnants of her spinnaker draped around her mast. We sauntered in astern of her scarcely able to believe our eyes.

The same gate produced another amusing incident which I did not witness, but was told about soon after. 'Onyx', the oldest gaff cutter of our little Jersey fleet was owned by Harry Fenn and kept in first class condition. She was one of those delightful old craft which not only sailed well given the right conditions, a fresh breeze on the beam, but also looked like a sepia photograph of the Victorian sailing craft off the south coast of England. Harry knew her well and often achieved good results in racing events.

'Onyx' had just entered Granville, but the lock gate was not yet open. Another Jersey yacht also awaited the opening of the gate so both skippers fastened their yachts bow and stern to each other and chatted while waiting. Soon the gate cracked open and Harry's companion, completely forgetting his stern mooring, cast off his bow rope to 'Onyx' and went ahead towards the slowly opening gate. The result was that 'Onyx' was carried forward and also swung towards the hinge of the gate where it met the granite wall. The long bowsprit soon wedged itself in the narrowing slot to the accompanying shouts of 'Onyx's' crew Harry knew that the gate was continuing to open and he also realised that not only would 'Onyx' break her bowsprit, but she could also lose her mast let alone what may happen to her hull if she stayed fastened there. The struggle was on and her crew ran forward and aft as they examined the position forward and tried to pull her free with the motor. At last, with no time to spare she was coaxed free with a rather damaged 'sprit, just in time to squeeze into the inner harbour.

It felt like midwinter, but it was just the end of another season with 'Dancing Lady' and we were thinking about laying her up. The club had held the laying up supper and the weather was steadily becoming colder, wetter and windier. I believe that cold winter winds of the same speed as a summer breeze always feel heavier in the sails of a yacht. Perhaps it is that the air being colder is more dense. However, in this October setting, someone from St Helier Yacht Club had accepted a challenge from Granville Yacht Club to play them at football. To get our team to the French port was no problem, several owners were asked to take those who were to play from Jersey aboard their yachts to Granville. I found that I had been given a small quota and Brian Slous and I set off with them in company with a small fleet early one saturday morning.

The weather was boisterous and we made good speed towards Granville under full sail to arrive midday. We went straight round to the Granville Yacht Club to determine what arrangements had been made. The match was to be played on sunday morning on a nearby football pitch, but tonight, tonight we were to dine with our hosts at a local hostelry. Not a good idea as we were to play a needle match in the morning. However! The meal was excellent and so was the company. Dudley, Brian and I got into conversation with a one armed dynamite manufacturer who, late in the evening, decided to show us his new property further north up the coast from Granville. The four of us set off into the night at high speed in a large Peugeot estate car driven with some élan by our host.

It was a complete 'take' from the then popular Maigret series. The headlights of the Peugeot theatrically lit up the tall gates of a country chateau and we found ourselves ushered to the top floor of this huge building. No, this was not the new property we were on the road to see, this was just an interlude en route to introduce us to a friend. I think it may have been a girlfriend who was a doctor on the staff of what turned out to be a huge psychiatric unit. We sat in a small bedroom, I was sitting on the bed near a handbasin strategically placed on the wall when drinks were offered or should I say drink in the singular, because a huge glass of good calvados was placed in each of our hands. I knew that this was impossible, we had just consumed a large meal and abundant supplies of wine followed by 'digestifs'. A full tumbler of calvados was not a good idea. You will recall the nearby handbasin? Well I am sorry to record that most of my drink, little by little, went down the drain. I remember wondering about the effect of calvados on lead plumbing.

Honour satisfied, we adjourned to the Peugeot and set off on the road once more. Our disabled host drove magnificently and showed no trace of having just consumed more than one glass of the firewater. At last we arrived right on the Normandy coast directly opposite to Jersey, lights a twinkling thirteen miles away across the sea. The new property was an old Napoleonic fort which was being converted into a large house, we admired the view from the car and thought, perhaps, that now we could go back to Granville and to bed. But no, we must come into the house for champagne!

A problem immediately emerged, try as we might, we could not find Dudley in the car. We opened all five doors and searched around both inside and nearby, but Dudley was nowhere to be found. There was no doubt that he had been in the car for he had been sitting next to me on the back seat. After a desultory search, we gave up and went inside whereupon our host found a packing case opener and set about opening a wooden box of champagne packed in straw. I gave in, the champagne was excellent and it was only three o'clock in the morning.

Some time later, as dawn was breaking, we returned to the patiently waiting car to find, sound asleep on the backseat, Dudley our long lost comrade of the night before! To this day no one ever discovered how it had happened, but it did not concern us too much then and accompanied by a snoring 'Houdini' we made our way south and back to Granville and our bunks.

Sleep was impossible and we soon found out that most of our team had been similarly knobbled. The result of the match played later on that Sunday was never for a moment in doubt. We were beaten. I wonder why?

I still carry a cameo memory of the dinner on the Saturday night, we had been served beautiful fresh trout still with their heads on and 'Nobby' Clarke got onto the long table at which we were seated to lead us all in 'Alouette'! Be that as it may, I felt chilled to the bone as 'Dancing Lady' thrust her bow out of the Granville inner harbour that Sunday afternoon and hit some huge seas rolling in across the shallows and backed by a strong westerly. We had reefed before leaving our moorings, but the wind was strong and the waves were steep. I was astern of 'Onyx' well handled as ever by Harry Fenn when he began to climb the face of one wave while we ran down the back of another. I found myself looking down the head of 'Onyx's' mast to her deck below so acute was the angle as she kicked up her bow in a welter of spray and we plunged down accelerating to the valley below.

As we reached deeper water the waves died down and we settled down to a brisk sail back to St Helier. Just off 'Taqhah's' port bow I watched her plunge her whole bow under rhythmically and repeatedly, the long bowsprit disappearing under the sea and gliding underwater like some large fish. 'Dancing Lady' was in her element and bowled along at a rate of knots and so we came quickly back to St Helier, our moorings and a good, long sleep that night.

In those days Granville was a lovely little seaside resort and fishing harbour. There was the usual market day once a week and a casino dating back to the period before the war. The streets and little squares were quaint and the people themselves very welcoming. Granville had long connections with the Channel Islands including during the German Occupation when many transport convoys set out for the Islands carrying German troops and equipment. I have written in my book 'Boys Remember More' about Captain Ted Larbalestier and his visits to Granville aboard the 'Normand', you may wish to look this up as it was an interesting interlude in Granville's long history. However, it is worth recalling in a little more detail the German raid on Granville early in 1945 when the port was in the hands of the American army.

Admiral Huffmeier was a leading Nazi among the higher ranking officers in the Kriegsmarine. It was he who was responsible for the planning and execution of the escape of the cruisers Scharnhorst and Gneisenau from Brest early on in the war. At the time of the invasion of Normandy in June 1944 he attempted a flanking attack on the invasion fleet employing for that purpose a mixed bag of German ships. Fortunately he was driven off after a severe mauling by the allied forces. It was a vainglorious attempt doomed to failure as Allied planning for the invasion had foreseen just such an attack.

Some of the remnants of the German ships made it back southward to St Malo, but three others sought refuge under the guns of Jersey and came into St Helier Harbour. There they lay unable to move for fear of air and sea attack if they ventured forth. Admiral Huffmeier had different ideas for their Marine crews and when it became apparent to him that they were to be absorbed into the Wehrmacht to form part of the garrison, he formulated a plan to attack the Allied forces now occupying the whole of the Normandy peninsula. It was to be a daring night attack, commando style and Granville was his target.

The American army had liberated the coastline around Granville and with only the Occupied Channel Islands to offer any source of concern, they let their guard slip. The little German fleet consisting of three ships was carefully prepared and manned by the Kriegsmarine sailors and in March 1945 slipped out of St Helier under cover of darkness. Their approach to Granville would have taken them between the south east coast of Jersey and the north of Chausey. Unobserved by the Americans they arrived off Granville and deployed ashore in inflatable boats. The German Marine Commandos had complete surprise on their side and took all of their objectives, blowing up fuel dumps and generally creating havoc.

At the Casino a dance was in full swing as the Germans burst in with blackened faces and well armed. There was so many American Officers present that they had to be careful about taking prisoners considering the limited size of the landing party and the available room on their ships. On their way back to their ships they found a prisoner of war camp holding German troops taken during the fighting in Normandy and 'liberated' them too. This turned out to be unwise as on arrival in Jersey and on reassignment to Units in Jersey, they gave an upbeat account of life with the Americans and thus lowered the morale of their comrades.

The German force had hoped to take prize some well laden shipping from the port, but only managed to take the 'Eskwood' a small coaster which was in ballast. Not unhappy with the night's events the German fleet returned to Jersey and to much celebration. As one looks around Granville today there is not much evidence of the war or of this little cameo fought out against the huge backdrop of the liberation of the whole of Europe. A very full account of this incident is to be found in the Jersey Occupation Society's archives.

On a much more minor note. I had sailed into Granville aboard a Contessa 32 with a good friend and fellow member of St Helier Yacht Club, John Smith and his wife, Marion. John was a leading architect on the Island and very good company. He had a strong sense of humour and always had a dry and witty comment for whatever befell. It was early evening on a calm night and we were just finishing a meal below when I heard a girl's voice repeatedly calling a boy's name. After a while I popped my head out of the main hatch to see what was happening. The girl was nearby and seemed quite distressed so I went onto the pontoon and asked her what was wrong.

She told me that five young people had set out from Gorey on the south east coast of Jersey in a Rigid Inflatable Boat and had swept into Granville at high speed. Safely ashore they had gone into the town and had eaten and drank perhaps a little unwisely of the plentiful supply of good French wine. The result had been that the boy who owned the R.I.B. had gone missing and she had come back to the harbour looking for him to find the boat gone from its place on the pontoon. She suspected that he had taken it out of the marina and I suspected that he was 'the worse for wear'.

I told her not to worry because as the tide was out he could not have left the marina. Some marinas have a high retaining cill which when the tide goes out retains some eight or ten feet of water, sufficient to kept the yachts afloat. With the retained seawater lipping the edge of the cill on the inside and the dry seabed on the outer side there was no chance that any boat would be leaving. It was then that we both heard a weak cry from somewhere high above us

By this time it was quite dark and try as we did we could not determine exactly where the sound was coming from among all the yachts, their masts and their rigging. We were certain however that it was not the cry of a seabird or other creature, but was human. The girl was now more than ever upset and, if indeed this was her missing boyfriend, I was going to need a dinghy. John was not anxious to dig out his inflatable, but a nearby English registered yacht immediately offered us theirs which was ready for use. The girl and I clambered in and set off quietly listening for the sound. At last we determined that it was coming from the top of a very high concrete caisson which formed part of the line of sea defences for the marina. A rusty steel ladder led to the top and, not anxious for the honour, I was about to tie off the dinghy's painter and climb the thirty feet or so of ladder to investigate the top when a head slowly emerged into view.

It was the missing boy. Slightly injured and badly shaken he made his way down the ladder to us with a little help and slumped into the bottom of the inflatable. His girlfriend very quickly examined him and spoke to him and his story of his night adventure was soon told. I was sure he was either on drugs or was drunk. He had left his friends in town without telling anyone and had made his way to the marina. Arriving alongside his R.I.B. he had decided to take it out for a spin and accelerating across the marina had failed to see that the smooth water he was travelling quickly over merged into the cill and then just darkness. There is always quite a lot of fairly bright lighting about a marina and this spoils your night vision so that when you leave a marina at night it takes a few minutes to adjust to the darkness offshore.

The R.I.B. careering along at a good few knots had hit the concrete cill and bounced up, skittered over the cement surface and the outboard motor had hit the inside edge of the cill rapidly decelerating the boat as the engine swung violently upwards. The craft and its driver fell forward and downward to the beach and stones below and while little real damage had been done to the rubber boat and its fibreglass hull, the same could not be said for its young driver. Probably the fact that he was drunk and relaxed saved him from more serious injury. Dazed, he could not understand where he was and had staggered across the wet sand, stones and seaweed towards the high retaining wall where he must have found another steel ladder and so we had found him at the top of the wall, befuddled, unsure of where he was or how to get down.

They were both very anxious not to call an ambulance, but I judged it highly desirable and they were whisked off. I returned the dinghy and thanked its owner. John was interested to hear what had been going on. The following morning, a much more composed girl arrived at the yacht to thank me. It seemed that the gendarmerie and port officials had now become involved and questions were being asked about the equipment or lack of it in their boat, no lifejackets, no flares and so on. This does happen from time to time. Usually it's a first boat and an owner, lacking in knowledge, fails to supply the vital equipment aboard. I heard no more, but I imagine that the young owner had been fined by the French authorities. The good news was that the boy had not been too badly hurt.

On a more amusing note. A rally of Westerly yachts, those fine little British cruising yachts, arrived in Granville and took places on the pontoons. They are virtually identical. The owner of one, a Centaur, had his young family aboard and after they had all dined at a restaurant in Granville it was agreed that the skipper would stay on in town to have a drink and a chat with other owners. His wife and the children walked back to the yacht and soon settled down for the night.

After having 'enjoyed' himself, the intrepid aforesaid skipper returned to his pride and joy and getting aboard entered the cabin as quietly as possible and undressing could not find his pyjamas where he normally kept them. Rummaging about he accidentally woke his crew only to find that they were not his crew. Wrong crew, wrong but identical boat!

Mike Smith sailed with Yvonne and me several times. Mike was, young well built, blond and handsome. Yvonne loved having him aboard. He was also very keen to sail and an excellent crew. I had met him through teaching when he was teaching craft at secondary level. Extremely popular with the students, the girls doted on him and the boys liked him for his direct manner and sporting ability. A love of motorbikes was the link between Mike and myself, we often nattered bikes for lengthy periods and he visited 'Northend Cottage', our home at that time with his latest 'toy', BMW, Yamaha or whatever had taken his fancy.

It was the race to Chausey and we were racing 'Blue Raven' our carvel hull Dutch built, cruiser. She was excellent in light airs as she carried a very tall mast in the American fashion. I was well crewed with both Yvonne and Mike and we made an excellent start in the 'B' division. Just clear of the startline, I decided to set the spinnaker and while Yvonne took the helm, I went forward with Mike and we soon had the spinnaker set on a broad reach. 'Blue Raven' got the bone between her teeth and surged forward. Yvonne, with good experience kept the sail nicely filled for an hour or so at which time we introduced Mike to helming with a spinnaker set. Do you think that he could keep that spinnaker flying?

After one or two gybes and loss of way, Yvonne kept helping Mike, but he just could not put together the necessary co-ordination to sail the yacht and at last had to surrender the tiller to Yvonne. Mike was not pleased to be outdone by a girl. After an interesting duel at the finish line with Dudley Harrison's 'Aegle', a very similar yacht, we took the gun and, well pleased with ourselves set off immediately from the south entrance to Chausey for Granville which lay shining in the evening sunlight. It had been a memorable day and having moored, the happy crew set off for the town to celebrate with the others.

After a good typically French meal and a glass of wine or two, Mike came over and said that he was 'going on' with some youngsters he had met and would be back late and not to wait for him. Would that be O.K? It was fine by us and I reminded Mike that he could enter the boat by the forward hatch straight into the forward cabin where he was occupying the port bunk in the two berth cabin. That way he would not wake Yvonne and me by coming through the main hatch and walking forward to his cabin. We separated and Yvonne and I, in high good humour after a wonderful day, went back to 'Blue Raven'.

The following morning I woke up bright and early and opening the main hatch and doors stood in the cockpit to enjoy the morning sunshine while the kettle heated up on the gas down below. A distant voice immediately called out to me. It was Mike on another yacht some distance off. "A fine mate you are," croaked Mike, "you gave my berth to someone else!" I was puzzled and told him that we had done no such thing. "Hold on a minute," I said and went down and forward to check just in case there was someone else – remember the skipper of the Westerly! The cabin was empty, but on one bunk was Mike's sleeping bag made up ready for use and on the other was his sailbag full of his 'gear'. Mike must have lowered himself down through the hatch and, not too clear about things after a 'night out' had mistaken his sleeping bag and sailbag for occupants of his cabin. Mike could not believe it when I told him, I think he still thought that we had given his berth to someone else! Was there something odd about sleeping in Granville?

BLUE RAVEN

At last the day came in the seventies when Yvonne and I began to let our eyes stray to other yachts. We were still happy with 'Dancing Lady' now a very different yacht from the cruiser we had bought from St Jean Birt and Hamish Mitchell. She had been re-rigged, set new sails and many improvements had been made aboard her, but we now looked at the lines of many faster and sleeker yachts.

The decision was made, we would sell dear old 'Dancing Lady' and replace her with something more up to date. So we advertised her privately in the classified columns of the Jersey Evening Post and soon had several inquiries. Our first would-be buyer seemed more than satisfied, a former civilian airline captain, he seemed to have all the right qualifications, but after an afternoon spent sailing 'Dancing Lady' things changed in an amusing way.

We were sitting around the saloon table, Yvonne, our 'buyer' and me, when having exhausted all the details of the purchase we came to negotiating the price. Suddenly our captain discovered that he had left the cat's food on the gas at St Aubin's where he lived and must needs leave posthaste. But he would be in touch immediately to conclude the bargain. We are still waiting for his phonecall many years later!

One or two other interested and more genuine people came, some fussed and came out with us for a sail then phoned with further questions, but at last a Mr Turpin arrived with his wife and the sale was so easy. They were delighted with the yacht and were willing to buy it. A cheque was made out there and then and Yvonne and I completed the transfer formalities for a British Registered Yacht with H.M.Customs who used to have an office on the Esplanade.

Not a little sad, but with a healthy bank balance we began our search for the 'replacement'. Most yachtsmen will admit to scanning the 'For sale' columns in the back of the yachting magazines, we devoured them. At last we decided that the best move was to take a holiday on the south coast and to search the harbours for yachts for sale, we could not then afford a new yacht for our little family absorbed much of our income. So we found ourselves camping in the New Forest in a lovely glade at Denny's Wood, living in our superb French frame tent. Nearby we parked our hire car which took us every day to new agents and to new creeks and moorings.

It was all very enjoyable. Little incidents kept us smiling. Sitting in a huge office furnished with leather chairs at Lymington with a lovely harbour view while the agent, who was also a property agent dealt with another client at his desk. Finding among the magazines on the coffee table Mike Peyton's book of sailing cartoons newly published by Hood the sailmakers, we laughed quietly and enjoyed his wry humour. "Laugh now," he wrote, "for it may soon happen to you." The agent looked up and smiled towards us, when we eventually sat at his desk the ice was already broken and we found a kindred spirit despite his grand office.

Another broker told us that the yacht we were interested in 'Tinkerbelle of Avalon', or some such high flown name, was away cruising and would be back on her moorings later in the month. That same day, while visiting a shipyard to examine another yacht which was mouldering away in the bushes behind a shed, we stumbled across 'Tinkerbelle of Avalon'. Paint had been stripped off her starboard side and the 'yard's men moved around it fitting and welding new plates to her steel hull where a huge hole had been gouged out by some rock or other. Some 'cruise', but a cautionary note to be digested as we continued our search.

We saw many yachts and for one reason or another decided against them one by one. Our 'new' broker had a most peculiar punched card system. He held a thick pile of index cards in his left hand and asked us a question about the type of yacht we were looking for, sail or power, length etc. Each time we answered he inserted a substantial steel pin into a hole on the edge of the stack and allowed cards to slip out of the pile and flutter to his desktop. After many questions he was left with only two or three cards and he began to read the details of available yachts from them. Do you know, his system worked, we found ourselves listening to descriptions of craft which met our fairly broad specification.

Armed with perhaps three addresses we set off with the children for a jaunt around Warsash and soon parked on the river near the Royal Thames Yacht Club. The club boatman ferried us

Illustration by
Peter Richards

out to 'Blue Raven' and as we approached her we liked what we saw very much. She was a lovely yacht of Dutch design and build of the 'Parader' class, elegant and well built. We were soon aboard her taking in all the details of a complicated little ship. We wanted a diesel engine, but she was fitted with a petrol engine. I decided to examine the installation to see if it was acceptable and removing the engine box found a perfect Morris Minor, four cylinder motor professionally converted for marine use. It was very quiet when started up and quite powerful at twenty-two brake horsepower. 'Blue Raven' suited us well with four berths in two cabins and many attractive features. The cockpit was much more exposed than 'Dancing Lady's' where we had sat well below and inside the coamings, now we were sitting level with the deck with marginal protection from the elements.

Notwithstanding minor faults, we liked her and decided to return to the broker's office. Once again he was very efficient and professional and knew all about the yacht on his books. Her owner was a very wealthy businessman living in the outskirts of Southampton. He had purchased 'Blue Raven' new some ten years earlier. But had used her very little and had now bought a new 'Dellquay Ranger,' a fast motorcruiser. The sailing yacht was for sale because having given her to his son to use the boy had given up on the idea after just one single-handed trip down the river. She had proved too much for him and he was not giving himself a fair chance to learn more.

Much to our surprise the price was almost within our budget and the broker suggested that we made an offer. We left his office and returned to the New Forest. We knew that the owner was unavailable for a few days and so we enjoyed walks and teas under the lovely trees of the forest. It was a perfect place. On Saturday morning we went into Lyndhurst, a pretty village nearby to phone our broker. I will always remember going to the phonebox in the main street and making that call. So much depended on it and soon I was through to the broker's office. Yes! Our offer had been accepted. We were thrilled and having celebrated with a cream tea we moved to completion very quickly.

The ensuing days were wonderful as we sorted out all the gear aboard 'Blue Raven' and cleaned and stowed everything. Her previous owner sent down extra sails and electronics we did not know went with her and was very helpful. It was an ideal transfer of ownership and the broker had certainly earned his fee.

Blue Raven

We moved camp from Denny Wood to 'Blue Raven' as soon as possible to find living aboard her was so much better than 'Dancing Lady'. The windows of armoured glass were large giving an excellent view and the finish of the interior was of the highest quality. We slept well that first night and woke up to a lovely misty view of the river.

I phoned Gordon Jones in Jersey, who was a good friend and knowledgeable yachtsman and he agreed to come over as soon as possible to sail our new possession back to St Helier. We were in no hurry, there was much to do to sort things out. It was not convenient lying on an open mooring in a trot of yachts and being ferried to and fro by the club's boatman. We found out that the Mercury Marina was nearby and that we could have a berth alongside a pontoon which we accepted. However, I was keen to see 'Blue Raven's' underwater area to check it for cleanliness and just to admire her lines. I also found that having a yacht lifted out around Warsash and the Hamble was a costly business.

From our trot I had noticed that when the tide was out there was a firm area of clean, fine gravel alongside a slipway just under the Royal Thames Yacht Club. Firmly fixed into this bed of gravel was one solitary thick stump of timber about ten feet tall. Our friendly boatman told me that the gravel beach and wooden post was once used by the old sailing barges for beaching and cleaning their underwater area. We were very used to 'drying out' in the Channel Islands so as we left our mooring under motor to go to the Mercury Marina, I made a detour and in the late afternoon tied up to the wooden post. As calculated the falling tide let us down gently onto the gravel and with her anchor chain along the starboard deck and boom swung out to heel her over. 'Blue Raven' nuzzled her post and rested quietly.

Because of other considerations we had to move her late in the day and so it was dark by the time the tide left her and we were ready to climb down onto the beach. The hull was very fouled and needed scrubbing off, but her keel and underwater area was a good as I could have wished for. Very few British yachts had drying legs, but I would make some for her at home and she would sit well on a drying mooring. We drove the car down the slipway and onto the beach and by the light of the headlights we set to. Her carvel hull was easily cleaned with stiff brushes and pails of water from the nearby river. Yvonne and I worked with a will while the children slept.

All of a sudden there was a white jacketed figure standing politely near us. His brass buttons shone in the car's headlights and his high collar and blue trousers indicated a uniform of some description. "Excuse me Sir, Madam," said this vision to our tousled and quite wet selves, "the members would like to invite you for drinks at the club" and he waved his arm in the direction of the Royal Thames. We looked in that direction and saw several figures gathered in one of the grand windows overlooking the river. "They are most intrigued by your cleaning off your hull on the beach," he concluded. We thanked him and accepted the invitation with the proviso that we would finish off and clean up before coming up to the club.

The warmth and grandeur of this fine club impressed us as we made our way through its portals. We, in our sailing gear, were swept in to the club to the same window area in which we had earlier seen the distant figures. Now they were real and close up, dressed in dinner jackets and with the ladies in evening dress quite a little crowd of the members made us most welcome. We were plied with questions on how we had moored there and other technicalities, it had seemed so normal to us to beach our yacht and to do this work. We had been taught well by the Jerseymen and now thought nothing of it, but to these ladies and gentlemen it was an unusual spectacle to see a yacht deliberately dried out for scrubbing off. "Well done both of you, dashed if I'm going to pay to have mine lifted out in future," was the general consensus, "Now tell me again, you lay your chain out…." We enjoyed a lovely moment in their company and we were later soon asleep aboard in the Mercury Marina.

What could I do about it? I had searched everywhere and I could not find the handle to operate the reefing gear and it was important to be able to reef the mainsail especially with such a tall mast. I reckoned that she would sail better under a slightly reefed mainsail around force four and I was certainly not going to cross the English Channel with all its variables of tide and wind without being able to reduce sail. I had found a large galvanised rigging screw in a locker which had no application to the yacht. I took it up to the mast and tried one end over the square key of the reefing gear, it was a good tight fit. Now if I could bend the rigging screw into a crank like a handle, this would do the trick.

I stepped onto the pontoon and set off to look for a workshop where I could borrow a large metalworking vice. There was a young man standing on the pontoon surveying the moored yachts, he looked a sailing man so I went up to him and asked if he knew where I could find a vice. He smiled, asked me what I wanted to do and gently took the rigging screw from me. "I had to do something like this once," he said and passing back the fitting gave me directions. "If anyone asks who gave you permission, tell them that Robin said it was O.K." I soon found the huge shed and bench and asked permission to use a vice. "Robin told you, did he," said the foreman, I asked him who Robin was. He grinned from ear to ear, "Why that's Robin Knox-Johnston, just back from round the world!"

Well everyone in yachting knew Robin, he was so famous for sailing 'Suahilli' round the world single-handed and I had not recognised him. On my way back to 'Blue Raven' after bending my rigging screw in a vice, I found Robin was still on the pontoon. He took the new 'reefing' handle from my hand and we had a long chat, the upshot of which was that I invited him to come to Jersey to give a series of talks to raise funds in aid of the Royal National Lifeboat Institution. Jersey was hoping to raise funds for a new lifeboat and Robin's talks would greatly assist in this. He readily accepted the invitation and came to the Island for five days as the guest of St Helier Yacht Club.

He is the most unassuming of men and well deserves his continued success in the sailing world as Sir Robert. I spent a lot of time organizing his visit, booking venues such as West Park Pavilion and arranging talks at schools let alone dinners and so on. It was at one large secondary school that I saw another side of Robin.

The school hall seating had been transformed into a large open square with a table in the middle for our speaker. Robin was so nervous that he was making heavy weather of his opening words when he began to describe opening a tin containing a birthday cake given to him by his mother. It was far at sea and Robin had been alone for weeks. The boys and girls warmed to him, they were no longer listening to a great national figure, but to a warm, human being. A hum of amusement and enjoyment ran around the teenagers and I saw Robin physically relax. At last he was enjoying himself. He told me later, that he would sooner sail twice round the world than face a large group of teenagers again. I didn't believe him. His visit to Jersey was a great success and the R.N.L.I. received a big boost to their funds.

'Blue Raven' was now ready for sea and Gordon arrived. He immediately strode across to another nearby pontoon and got a good full sideview of her. In his lovely Welsh accent he breathed, "Boy, she's a yacht." I asked Gordon to be the skipper for he had a great deal more navigational experience than I and it is wise to defer to superior knowledge especially at sea! We set off in the late afternoon as the tide served and rendezvoused off Lymington with 'Blue Raven's' former owner who had kindly offered us the use of one of the new liferafts, an uncommon feature aboard a yacht in the seventies. He steamed alongside in his new Dellquay Ranger and we chatted for a while before he took off in a flurry of spray.

We cruised under sail off the south coast of the Isle of Wight on course for the Casquets and enjoyed our gallant little yacht's performance. We had never seen her sail before and she immediately reminded me of the Dragon 'Lalun'. She had the same driving quality where she never seemed to slow down and hobbyhorse as some yachts do when breasting a swell. The balance of the sails with the design of the hull was so right. We were making fine progress towards the Channel Islands.

Crossing the shipping lanes in the early evening light, we had wonderful views of the great ocean-going cargo ships and tankers. Some were of enormous size, especially when viewed from the open cockpit of a thirty foot yacht. We left the Casquets to starboard and picked up the 'Race' off the Normandy coast and also ran into light winds and thick fog.

Our little Morris engine purred away as we motored through the fog and made the required warning sounds on our mouth blown trumpet. After a while we detected the sound of a heavy engine beating not far off on our bow, we increased our vigilance. Eventually, where the fog must have lifted a little, we saw the multiple display of lights of a tug with a tow astern of it. The tug was towing Moitessier's trimaran towards Cherbourg and we passed clear astern.

As the sun rose we warmed up after the chill and dampness of the night and had an early breakfast provided by Yvonne. The fog had drifted away and left us with a good view of the coast of Normandy. We skirted south of Sark and rounded Grosnez on the north coast of Jersey. It was only then that I realised just how tired I was with all the days of preparation and now no sleep for a whole night. I had the helm just north of the Rigdon Bank when I distinctly knew that an aircraft was taking off just astern of us and would pass low overhead in a moment. My mind was playing tricks, but otherwise I felt just fine and there was St Ouen's Bay and an easy passage home to a mooring in St Helier Harbour.

Gordon was as pleased as we were and his planning of our trip had been spot on. Yvonne had a pint beer tankard engraved for Gordon with a picture of 'Blue Raven' on it and a little cloud of fog just at its masthead.

I made wooden beaching legs for 'Blue Raven' and well remember the night she took the ground on her new mooring in St Helier Old Harbour. Because of work commitments, I could not let her ground during the day, so I decided to sleep aboard her and she would ground during the night. No two yachts settle down on the beach in quite the same way. Some are way down by the bow or at any other angle including stern down and they can be quite uncomfortable to be aboard because of the slope of the deck and cabin sole. I waited in my bunk, dozing lightly, I cocked an ear for any sound and at last felt her gently touch the beach. I need not have worried, she was just fine, leaning slightly and her weight on one leg while the other was clear of the mud by two inches, the correct set up. A yacht must never take the ground on both legs sharing the load as the strain of the weight of the hull in this position can be very great.

So began a long association with a lovely yacht which cruised quickly under sail and was responsive to her helm. The little Morris Minor engine proved to be reliable and started easily, an important feature in a sailing yacht around the Channel Islands where tidal currents are strong and reefs abound. If you are sailing in light winds and the tide is pushing you down onto a reef, you need a reliable engine to see you clear of danger.

Lightly crewed with Yvonne and I and the young girls, she was easy to handle compared with 'Dancing Lady' and although she did not have the auxiliary engine power of our former diesel engined yacht, she had adequate power. The crew increased for racing and we were nearly always 'four up' for round the bay and longer distance racing. Good friends such as Brian Slous, another craftsman in wood and the Channel Islands snooker champion, Norman Luce, a business man and owner of a school supplies company and former boatbuilder in New Zealand and Graham Talbot who was the St Helier Yacht Club secretary were often aboard. And there was others too who gently unfolded their characters as we sailed and chatted and they showed their metal around the deck.

A good team aboard a yacht is an experience which is difficult to repeat in other areas of civilian life. The services often develop team spirit and there are businesses which encourage teamwork as well as certain sports, but the slow development of the crew aboard a small yacht is something quite different. There are long periods when racing a yacht when there is time for chat and much laughter, but there are other times when the race is 'needle' and you can feel the tension. Perhaps it is as you come down on a difficult mark of the course, a buoy with the tide streaming away from it with a tail of foam on the water to guide you, or during the start of a race on the line with many yachts under sail 'negotiating' for the best starting position.

There was one winter race around the buoys which we should have easily won, but did not. Nobody else won it, so that's not too bad. The wind was very light and on about the third mark of the course we were well placed as the wind fell lighter and most yachts found that they could not lay this windward mark and abandoned the race. With her tall mast catching the lightest zephyr, 'Blue Raven' was doing well. The crew lay still about the deck as I nursed her at about two knots towards the large red iron buoy. There was a stillness and silence aboard which bespoke the tension as our eyes strained forward comparing our bow with the buoy and the sky, trying to determine whether we would round the mark or just fail as the tide carried us downwind. Suddenly, Norman Luce stood up alongside the cockpit and declaimed in his New Zealand twang, "No, we're not going to make it, that's it!" "Shut up and get down Norman." I hissed, not taking my eye off the red target. Norman folded up and settled down quietly, we could hear the lap of the tiny bow wave and feel the sails pulling just a little as we came within feet of the rusty iron, seaweed encrusted buoy. We could smell it. I sensed the crew were waiting to shove it off with the soles of their deck shoes. We crept up closer and closer, at last the bow was alongside it, would the midships, wider section also go through. Yes, with hardly any clearance I drew the tiller up to windward and 'Blue Raven's' stern moved away from risk of touching and we were round. No other yacht had made it.

We could not lose, or so we thought. We had time to look around to see all the other yachts making back to St Helier as the light breeze and tide took us down to the next and penultimate mark of the course. Quickly there, we rounded it easily and cracked out the spinnaker with the wind now well aft of the beam, it filled and looked lovely, well filled and rounded. Then I noticed that the nearby land at Belcroute Bay was moving in the wrong direction ever so slowly. It should have been moving alongside us away towards our stern, it wasn't. We were sliding slowly astern towards a partially covered reef at Noirmont Point as the tide moving slightly faster than the breeze moved us, took us backwards.

We tried everything, trimming the sails, redistributing our weight about the deck, still we moved backwards in a dying breeze. I slid open the little Perspex cover over the engine instrument panel in the cockpit and put the gearlever into place.

I pulled out the choke knob and made sure the ignition key was in place. We could now hear the trickle of the sea as it ran across the top of the reef, still we made way astern and still the spinnaker stood. At last I pressed the starter button while glancing over the stern at a head of rock just below the surface and so close. The engine purred into life, we did not. We had abandoned the race. What a good crew they were.

THE MOORINGS

Long before marinas and pontoons existed and still today, many yachts took the ground or beach when the tide went out, twice each day. Some boats were allowed to lie down on their sides with the need to secure everything aboard while still afloat. Others were designed with flat bottoms so that they stayed more or less level, but the majority were fitted with legs, commonly made of wood. The legs allowed the hull of the yacht to lean just a little to port or to starboard, to have stood on both at the same time would have put a tremendous strain on the hull.

Nobody had a good word to say about legs. They were heavy to handle, slippery when wet and cluttered the deck when at sea, if you carried them with you. Often they were left in the dinghy which had carried the crew out to the yacht and which was now tied to the moorings. If you came in a little too late onto your mooring as the tide was dropping, panic could ensue as you rushed to 'acquire' the legs and to get them on. They were usually secured by a bronze through bolt which meant threading the bolt through a small hole in the yacht's side and having someone down below to fix and turn down the wing nut. If you were single-handed, well you probably had evolved some means of holding the leg in place. The buoyant wooden leg loved to float up sideways and took some effort to control and to submerge them. And, of course there was the matter of the fore and aft guy ropes to be secured for each leg, wet, sometimes muddy and carrying seaweed, legs were not fun.

Should you by misfortune allow a yacht to fall over while fitted with her legs, the result was usually disastrous. The foot of the leg would be forced inwards towards the keel and the leverage would pull on the well fastened upper part breaking out the side of the hull as it submerged, perhaps on a falling tide. Disaster enough if you were on your moorings in St Helier Harbour, but more so if, for instance you were in Chausey Sound.

Such a misfortune befell Noel Romano, a local grower. His plywood hulled yacht came down on an uneven or soft patch of sand and falling over broke open the side of his thirty foot yacht. It was beyond the ability of his limited crew to repair this before the tide returned, but several other yachtsmen immediately dropped everything and contrived to remove the leg and to fasten a piece of plywood over the damaged area. She floated on the rising tide and was later repaired in Jersey.

I had a similar experience again in Chausey Sound with 'Blue Raven'. I had a crew of four friends aboard when we took one of the Granville Yacht Club's mooring buoys after a cruise down to the islands. It was a spring tide and I had miscalculated the effect of this so that as we retired for the night so did the tide and we began to 'take' the ground and to lean over ever so gently to port. I hoped that the yacht would only lean a little, but I was seriously disappointed as she went over further and further and at last lay on her side at an extreme angle. There was to be little

The Moorings

chance of sleep. Fortunately we had come down on clean sand although there were rocks and stones all around. There was nothing to do, but to wait and to turn off all the valves on the side of the hull.

The rising tide gently surrounded us and rose up to cover the side deck and began to lip the cockpit coaming, but 'Blue Raven' did not stir. I began to feel alarmed. Perhaps I should have fastened a sail or cover over the cockpit! Suddenly she lifted and continued to rise steadily. Afloat again and on an even keel I felt an enormous sense of relief.

We were aboard 'Dancing Lady' and at that time our mooring was on a row of yachts among several rows of them in the town harbour, jus below the former Weighbridge in St Helier. Preparing to leave the moorings and struggling with the legs we heard the beat of an approaching yacht's motor. It was 'Doc' Curran aboard his new Polish built Folkboat. The Folkboats were a popular new class of small cruising yacht, designed in Scandinavia, they were clinker planked and had something of the lines of a fat dragon, they sailed quite well. British built Folkboats had a neat cabin, but little headroom inside. The Polish built boats had attempted to cure this by fitting a high cabin quite out of scale to the yachts hull. It was practical, but ugly. Being imported from communist Poland, they were also reasonably priced.

In common with other Polish Folkboats, 'Doc' Curran's was fitted with a single cylinder diesel engine and the gear lever was a huge bar sticking straight up out of the cockpit floor just aft of the cabin. We watched as he approached his mooring, his crew, Tony Chinn, waiting alert with the boathook on the foredeck ready to sweep up their buoy in a single flashing stroke as 'Doc' slowed her by going astern. But, hello, was he going a little too fast. Slow up 'Doc' we thought, now all eyes attentive waiting for a bit of fun. Yes, much too fast, five knots at least! Tony swept up the buoy in great style to find himself running down the starboard side of the little yacht at great speed, five knots to be exact calling to his skipper to go astern. He managed to divest himself of the buoy at the stern of the yacht alongside 'Doc' just as we thought he was going to go for a morning dip.

As the yacht swept past us turning dramatically to port at a speed at which I would not have cared to negotiate the surrounding moorings, we had a clear view of the helmsman hanging on to the gear lever in an attempt to move it. Round they went in a great arc smoothing the water alongside her as she swept around. Tony regained the foredeck and they approached the mooring buoy once more in fine style. Was Tony now looking a little nervous as he kept glancing back towards the cockpit? Still at five knots, once again the foredeck hand caught the buoy with the boathook and once again left the foredeck in some haste to release the buoy just before the deck finished, however, the boathook was not so lucky and sailed through the air to land in the water with a splash. We now saw the ill fated skipper with both hands firmly clasped around the top of the gearlever and both feet planted firmly on the cabin bulkhead trying and failing to shift it.

He quickly abandoned this posture as the line of boats ahead came hurtling towards him. The little Folkboat responded to full rudder gallantly and just missed the assembled sterns of the moored yachts. Away went 'Doc' again. But this time he continued away from us only to return a little later at about two

The Moorings

knots quietly and easily onto his mooring. It transpired that when the little single cylinder engine was pulling hard, it distorted the wooden engine bed and the gearbox would jam in gear somehow. Less throttle and all was well. We all had things to learn about our little boats.

'Minivet' was a little tub of a yacht, she was about twenty feet long, but looked short and fat. The balance between her width, freeboard and overall length was not right in my opinion. She was off the board of a good designer, Fred Parker and had been built by Woodnutts on the Isle of Wight so she should have been just fine, but….I was on the moorings in the lines of moored yachts just below the windows of St Helier Yacht Club, Yvonne and I were preparing to set out in 'Lalun' our Dragon when our attention was attracted towards 'Minivet'. Her new owner, a science teacher from a local grammar school, was also preparing to leave his moorings. He had just bought her and his young son of about fourteen summers was also aboard. The boy had been told off to stand at the bow and to attend to the forward mooring and to release it, to throw it overboard when requested.

Dad was tinkering about in the cockpit, trying to start the small engine which was declining all entreaties to perform. The skipper was getting exasperated and his son was getting fed up with all this hanging about holding onto a stupid bit of rope. Obviously a boy with a short fuse, he reached explosion point and just threw the rope angrily away over the bow where it sank out of sight. The consequence of course was that the little yacht began to swing and to move backwards under the weight of the stern moorings still attached. Glancing up briefly from his 'duties' around the engine box, Dad suddenly noticed that the scenery had changed somewhat and that with no engine power and no sails up he was about to collide with yachts astern of him.

'Like father, like son' is quite a well-known truism. Short fuse too, Dad's temper exploded and rushing along the side deck of the little yacht he reached the bow in less time than it takes to write this line and pushed his son over the bow into the water where he too sank out of sight. So now we had a little yacht without crew, but with an irate skipper lying neatly across the bows of other yachts. We didn't wait to see how the situation developed further. It didn't augur well for future trips out in the bay.

I had decided to take 'Blue Raven' off her mooring at high water on a spring tide to dry her out high up on the beach in the Old French Harbour not far from my own moorings. It was very early on a lovely summer morning no one was about as yet and the yachts little petrol engine purred happily as 'Blue Raven' and I wended our way through the line of yachts. Nearing the temporary mooring I suddenly noticed that a very big motoryacht named 'Alfay' was well below the water, only her cabin top and bow projected above the sea. She had sunk overnight on her mooring. With the big tide about to drop, I realised that all that water enclosed within 'Alfays' hull would burst her open with its sheer weight.

'Alfay' was a former 'Fairmile' or similar class motorboat built for the services during the war. She was of wooden construction made up of laminates diagonally laid in several layers with canvas and white lead between them. She had three large diesel engines which were just being replaced with new ones by her owner Alfie Regal. Alfie was a major builder on the

The Moorings

Island involved in several large contracts, but 'Alfay' was his pride and joy.

I quickly tied off 'Blue Raven' alongside the sunken yacht and crossed onto her. Looking through the cabin windows I could see all round the stripped out interior, for fitting new engines is a major operation on a yacht. The seawater was well above the engines which glinted in the morning light below the water. What to do? The need to pump her out as the tide fell was obvious, but a very big pump would be required for this job. Who would have one? The shipyards, but they were shut and the tide would have dropped before they opened. The Fire Service came into my mind like a flash. I would have to get to a phone and quickly. I jumped aboard 'Blue Raven' and quickly fitted her legs, I didn't want two disasters. I was just untying the dinghy to row ashore to find a phone when I heard footsteps on the nearby road.

It was one of the yard men making his way to South Pier to open up. I called out to him and pointed out the problem with 'Alfay'. "Go to the phone, dial 999 and ask the Fire Service to bring pumps to save her," I shouted. He was off and in next to no time the brilliant firemen were there. No fuss, they understood the problem and borrowing a nearby boat had a big petrol auxiliary pump aboard 'Alfay' in no time at all. They were enjoying themselves. It was just in time as 'Blue Raven' and 'Alfay' were now taking the ground.

Seawater cascaded from the big pump, but not satisfied with the volume of water, the firemen fetched another pump. I went to the phone, it was still early morning and looked up Alfie Regal's home number. It was a sleepy voice which answered the phone, but it was Alfie. I explained the situation and the action which I had taken and Alfie was wide awake! He was soon standing on the sodden deck of 'Alfay' with me, shaking my hand and telling me that I was his best friend ever as the pumps roared and gushed.

What had caused her to sink was that Alfie's own men who were installing the new engines had disconnected the three large exhaust pipes at the stern leaving three holes of about four inches diameter in the stern of the yacht just above the waterline. The yacht was lying on the beach on the dry sand at a good stern down angle and as the tide had come up the sea had entered the stern easily and flooded her. The engines were removed, the stern holes plugged with wooden bungs and canvas, as they should have been and I began work on 'Blue Raven'.

'Alfay' survived after much work on the interior and on the engines and was often used by her owner. Years later she was sold to a new owner who kept her in Brittany on the river Rance, but she is still about as an old hulk, dried out on a riverbank somewhere. 'Sic transit.'

'Point One' was a magnificent launch, more than thirty feet in length she was a 'one off', specially built for her very wealthy owner and based on the famous Fairey Swordsman high speed yachts. I remember going aboard her when she first arrived in Jersey waters and being amazed at her vast open plan accommodation. Cork surfaces on the bulkheads and terracotta colour schemes set off the light and airy interior, she was built for day use and had little or no sleeping accommodation. Her performance on large diesel inboard engines was of racing calibre for a fast yacht in those days.

The Moorings

Because of her performance, it was agreed with the harbourmaster that she should be given a deepwater mooring just inside the pierheads and below the old lifeboat shed. This meant that unlike all the other yachts she was not tide bound and could go and come regardless at any time, a considerable advantage, but on one condition. She was to be available to an emergency lifeboat crew for high speed rescue work when the much slower lifeboat was unsuitable. This condition was agreed to very willingly by her owner as there was no marina and therefore no pontoons at that time.

The day came when 'Point One' was needed, skindivers had got into difficulties off St Catherine's Breakwater, the large granite quay which reached out many hundreds of feet from the south east coast of the Island. A strong current and turbulence over the rocks had dragged two divers away from the back of the breakwater and towards the open sea. An emergency crew was quickly aboard, and relishing the chance to see what their high speed craft could do they set off in great style from St Helier Harbour eastbound for St Catherine Breakwater. Now they had a choice, the long way round outside the great reef of rocks which lies to the south east of the Island leaving the Demie des Pas tower and all dangers to port or the much quicker, more tricky, but well used route through the 'Gutters'.

Gutters, as you know are channels made of manmade materials such as galvanized iron, cast iron, plastic nowadays and conduct water along a defined path. The old sailors who explored the reefs south east of the Island knew the routes they had discovered through the rocks as the 'Gutters' a very apt name though they were not manmade or as accommodating as galvanized iron, but were solid and craggy granite. It was a brave skipper who decided on the quicker route at such high speed where correct positioning of the boat on marks and transits was vital. To be quite sure, one crewman went forward and courageously stood in the bow, hanging on to the stainless steel pulpit and keeping a lookout for any dangers.

High speed and rocks lying just under the surface of the sea, possibly concealed by the light conditions, are not a good combination and sure enough 'Point One' struck a rock with her propellers and rudders. The brackets holding the shafts and the propellers were torn away and the stern of the yacht rapidly filled with water and now it was the turn of the emergency crew to radio for assistance.

There is a law somewhere in physics to do with objects, movement and deceleration, at least if there is not, the crewman on the bow discovered one. For when 'Point One', in the way of such things, stopped suddenly, his grip on the pulpit was torn off and he went over the bow and into the water rather quickly. I discount rumours that were spread about at the time that he bounced along on the surface of the sea as does a flat stone skimmed by a boy!

'Point One' was rebuilt after she had been salvaged and remained in Jersey waters, but was sold. We now have high speed, Rigid Inflatable, inshore lifeboats for such work. One such lifeboat is kept at St Catherine's where her skilled crew often effect rescues off the south east coast and its dangerous reefs.

ON LEAVING YOUR YACHT

This is not so much about how to tie up or moor a yacht, but more to do with thinking before you leave any yacht or boat when at sea. Why do I think I should write about this? Well perhaps if you bear with me and read on you may think that it was worthwhile.

I was chatting with a former honorary chief of police, Frank Marquer quite recently who owned a well-equipped fishing boat, a Channel Islands 22 named 'Seajay'. He told me that he was sitting in the stern preparing some mackerel he had just caught while two or three miles off Corbière. The sea was quite calm and there was only a light breeze, when a wave passed under his boat causing it to roll and throwing him over the side into the sea. One minute he was sitting there and the next he was struggling in the sea looking across a fair distance to his boat.

The boat's gear box was fortunately in neutral so that it was not moving away from him at any speed, but it was certainly drifting away in the light breeze. Just an easy swim you may think, then climb aboard. Not a bit of it. He began to swim in his clothes and it took all his strength, not stopping for a moment, just to catch up with it. Had he delayed or rested he may not have made it at all. He believes that a nylon shirt he was wearing may have assisted his sudden exit

When you are aboard a small boat, you feel very close to the sea, but when you reach up from the water when you are in it alongside a boat you realize that you have a problem. How can you haul yourself aboard in heavy wet clothing . Sometimes the stern offers the best chance of getting aboard. There may be a ladder or the rudder may offer a foothold, even an outboard motor may give you that first lift out of the sea. One thing is certain, if you make it you will breathe a sigh of relief and vow not to let that happen again.

There are of course, many good solutions to this problem. Do not go out on your own perhaps; not always can you find someone to accompany you. Always wear a safety harness; not very convenient when you want to handle some fishing gear or to slip down below for something. Fit a ladder or steps and perhaps plan what you might do to make boarding your craft from the sea easier. Remember that even if you do have someone with you that they might not have the strength to help you aboard. What can you do then? Tie them alongside and motor gently to the shore; use a halliard from the mast and a winch; inflate the dinghy and use that as a boarding platform maybe?

It will never happen to most sailors so why bother. It was beautiful day off Granville and the pretty French yacht was hardly sailing in just the merest zephyr of a breeze. The sun shone down and the young couple in the yacht's cockpit thought of cool drinks and cool winds. They had eloped the day before and were now sailing aimlessly down the nearby Normandy coast.

On Leaving Your Yacht

The breeze died completely. They dived down below and folding their clothes neatly, scrambled up into the cockpit and plunged into the welcoming cool sea. They laughed and played in the deliciously cool water alongside their yacht with hardly a care in the world.

They had not thought to lower the sails, after all, there was no wind at all. Coming up invisibly across the water was a light breeze heralding the returning wind. The sails shook and filled gently and the yacht gathered way. Suddenly aware of the yacht's movement they swam casually after it no doubt amused at first, but then they realized with growing horror that they could not catch up with it, try as they might.

The attention of a passing yachtsman was drawn to a little yacht which seemed to be sailing oddly. He passed close by and seeing no crew he called out to see if there was someone below. On getting no reply he boarded her with his crew and found two neatly folded piles of clothing. If only one of them had stayed aboard while the other swam or even if a light line and a buoy had been kept at hand. Dropping the sails alone would not have guaranteed a safe return to a small yacht when a breeze pushes her along. The bare mast can be an effective 'sail'. It was a very sad event and a timely warning to all sailors no matter how big or small their yacht.

Johnnie Thuillier and I were talking about the 'Marie Celeste' some years ago and speculating about what may have happened to her crew, for you will recall that all of them had disappeared from a well found sailing ship. It is one of the great mysteries of the sea. John recalled a similar incident off Cork in southern Ireland when he was a boy. A fair sized three masted sailing ship had been seen off the coast and it was presumed by the coastguard that she was coming into Cork Harbour. However, she was not flying the appropriate signal flags requesting a pilot, saying who she was or that she was free of disease.

Feeling that something was amiss, for through their 'bring 'em nears' the local fishermen could see no sign of sails being lowered preparatory to entering port, a boat set off to find on boarding the ship that there was no crew to be found on her. She was brought into the harbour and examined. Her cargo of copra was intact and there was no sign of any problem. This, like the mystery of the 'Marie Celeste' was never solved.

The Royal Navy Sailing Association yacht was quite small, but adequate for her crew of four young officers. She was being tied up in the morning sunlight at the top of a spring tide which was barely a foot below the edge of the quay. Nearly forty feet of water would have to drain out through the pierheads in six hours before the yachts and fishing boats would once again take the ground and dry out. Now the crew were quickly organizing themselves for a jaunt into St Helier and no doubt a pink gin or two.

I paused beside them and we chatted. It was their first cruise and they had come straight down from Dartmouth. Could I offer them a lift into St Helier. This was readily accepted. While they got ready, I fetched my car and waited while they all got in, much to my surprise. "How long are you going to be in town?" I asked. "Oh, just the morning I think," was the reply. "So is no one staying aboard?" "She's quite safe there isn't she?" I explained to them that the tide was dropping fast and that by the time they reached St Helier their yacht would be straining on her mooring lines as she hung from the harbour wall before falling to the beach perhaps another twenty feet below her keel. A rapid discussion followed and three came with me while one stayed aboard.

It was way back in the early 50's when Don Filleul purchased an open fishing boat from Guernsey. There had been a cursory examination of the hull and equipment by Don and his two partners before the deal was done. Later in Jersey, they found that water was leaking into the hull from a hidden source. Nothing daunted, they took their boat to a shed and dismantled the extra planking which formed a protective shield to prevent lobster pots and their gear from damaging the hull itself. They soon found that their prize boat had been crushed by a cargo boat while in St Peter Port harbour and that the 'protective planking' was nothing other than a bodge.

Being young and enthusiastic, they set to and re-ribbed their hull and carried out other repairs. Now they were ready to go fishing! However, the evening fishing in and around St Aubin's Bay was disappointing. They had to fish late in the day because of work commitments and had thought that this time of day would have yielded good catches. Not so.

Returning from yet another failed fishing trip they saw a bright light shining ahead of them and on drawing closer found a fishing boat with a bright lamp suspended above the water at its stern. This must be the solution to their problems, a bright lamp equals lots of fish thought Don & Co. Still elated with the idea of a powerful lamp, the morning light found Don at G D Laurens Hardware and General Store in Queen Street. He was shown a fine Tilley lamp in chromium plated brass available for a princely sum. The purchase was made. Now for the fish!

That evening on their favoured fishing ground the three lads unearthed their new 'secret weapon' from within its packaging and discarding the maker's instruction leaflet set about lighting up. Ignorant of what fuel it burned, they had fortunately bought paraffin and not petrol and now they slopped a generous measure into and about the lamp in the 'ideal' conditions of a rocking small boat.

The match was struck and soon the Tilley lamp was lit. Too well! Flames enveloped the whole lamp and threatened the safety of the boat and its crew. "Throw it overboard," Don yelled. Unfortunately no one had thought to tie a line to the lamp so as it hit the water it sank quickly still glowing beneath the waves. Don went on to own fine motor yachts which gave him much pleasure, but his eyes glinted with a fond recollection as he retold this story.

The sea and all things to do with it and on it are one great continuous lesson. You can never know it all, but you can try to learn a little of its lore.

SPLASH AND SPLOT

My brother, Francis, had every reason to be pleased with himself. The sun was shining down on us as we lay just below the club windows, we had come back from a lovely sail around the bay in his newly acquired Dragon 'Lalun'. I had only just met Yvonne and Margaret and the three of us were crewing for Francis. Our skipper cast his eagle eye around the deck, but hello, he did not like that making fast of the bow mooring on the little bollard. His newly acquired, chromium plated, bronze, maltese cross shaped bollard had a bow line wound around it in a less than satisfactory pattern. He strode forward along the narrow deck, careful to hold onto the rigging as he passed it for there were no stanchions and lifelines on a Dragon.

"Look here, you three," he said in a happy tone of voice. We immediately forgathered forward anxious not to miss some new piece of 'marlinspike' seamanship about to be demonstrated to us. Francis knelt down over 'his' precious bollard, undid the offending rope and quickly remade it in a neat pattern. "There," he said, "that's how it's done, and that's how I'd like to see it done in future." Satisfied with establishing his position and having demonstrated his higher level of authority and knowledge in such matters, he stood up and took a selfsatisfied step backwards….and disappeared over the bow and out of sight, underwater! What an exit, by the way, a little advice to budding crew, learn to suppress a snigger when you feel one coming on and never laugh outright at your skipper's minor failings.

But such events are not uncommon, 'Cap On It' Bisson was manning the bow of 'Speedwell', a fine six meter style yacht, when he saw the need to use the boathook to help her pass along the seawall as she neared the Victoria Pier. The sun was very bright though it was early in the morning. Long deep shadows lay everywhere on the still water of the inner harbour and the little yacht was a pleasant sight to watch as she slid under good control past all nearby obstructions.

A touch with the boathook here and there saw the yacht through, but here suddenly was the harbour wall, a little too close 'Cap On It' reached out with the boothook and followed it right over the bow and into the water as it passed right through the deep shadow which a moment before had looked so like a granite wall. His skipper Reg Nicolle was more than a little surprised.

I had been to church on a Sunday morning and at about ten o'clock came down to the South Pier in my car to check my dinghy. The dinghy was quite special, it was a Lymington Scow, a delightful little sailing boat which I had recently acquired and which doubled as a harbour punt. A good friend, Father James Hargreaves, the parish priest of that lovely granite church in St Aubin's village, The Sacred Heart, had told me that he wished he had a little boat to go out in occasionally. I had responded by sailing the little Scow across the bay a day or two later and giving it to him to use. Weeks later, he returned it to the South Pier and had phoned me to say where it was and thank you.

I was wearing a suit and there was the dinghy in a bad position left tied alongside the granite steps leading down to the water with her painter disappearing straight down and the bow already beginning to follow it. She had been tied up too low down and was about to swamp. There was no time to change my clothes for sailing gear. I hurried down the steps and stepped onto the little curved deck just forward of the mast and grabbed hold of the mast. I knew immediately that I was in trouble. The little bow went down further with my weight and, worst of all, the dinghy began slowly and steadily to roll over away from the harbour wall towards the still, deep water behind me. I was clinging onto the mast and the inevitable was about to happen.

Above me I heard Terry Ashborn laugh out loud with delight as he saw my predicament and impending doom. No help was forthcoming, but suddenly I realised that a well laden punt with four men sitting in it was passing just behind me. I quickly released my grip and fell backwards into the punt across the laps of its occupants. They were somewhat surprised by my arrival as the freeboard of their craft moved from three inches to two, but they reached the ladder and I was soon, dry and not a little relieved, standing on the pier once more. I could hear Terry scoffing and shouting, "You jammy bu**er!" That was a near one and a little bit jammy perhaps.

The Sea Cadets had a wonderful unit operating out of Fort Regent that fine old fortress overlooking St Helier. They were very active and operated two long rowing gigs off a mooring at the far end of the Old Harbour, just below the Weighbridge. On Sunday mornings they had a church parade inside their quarters at the Fort when Officers and 'men' were turned out in their number one uniforms. The gigs had been in use on Saturday and had been left afloat in the harbour and now it was time to see them back onto their mooring side by side.

Two young sailors complete with bell-bottom trousers and navy tunics were ordered off to move the boats. They were soon aboard and sculled the long craft up the harbour where they secured them. Now they had to wait for the tide to fall so that they could walk ashore. They waited patiently, chatting idly as they sat on the strong grey painted thwarts, until at last the falling tide had left the mooring.

Walk ashore, it was deep mud all around the boats. The Royal Navy spirit to the rescue. The taller of the two lads slipped off his shoes and socks and hanging them round his neck slipped over the side with rolled up trousers and slithered towards his chum who now stood up on the gunwhale ready to sit on his friend's shoulders for a 'piggyback' ashore. He got up alright and his friend took several difficult steps alright, but then with a sudden skid both fell flat backwards into the deep, black mud. I will draw a veil over their appearance as they struggled to regain their feet!

It happens that as yachts leave their drying moorings under power and usually when the craft has just floated, that the propeller is fouled by a mooring rope. In the normal way of things, this usually happens when the crew is in a hurry to be off. Just a few revolutions of the propeller when it is close to a rope is enough to draw it in and there you are, moored by a rope you

Splash And Splot

cannot reach. Then begins the trials and experiments to see how the offending rope may be removed. You try revolving the propeller shaft ahead or astern, sometimes by hand. You may even get into the water and duck down over the overhanging stern to find the propeller almost beyond reach embedded in a tight ball of heavy rope. You may be lucky and clear the rope, but it will have taken time and you may be very wet. Not a good start to that little cruise you were planning or you may be late over the line at the start of a race.

Dudley looked very elegant in the early morning light sporting a new 'Jersey'. The 'Jersey' is a particular knitted garment quite unlike the ordinary pullover and has its Guernsey counterpart. The knit is of heavy, high quality wool, the neck is not like a crew neck, but more of a slot with ribbing at the front and back. Some 'Jerseys' also have an anchor knitted into the front and they were the traditional wear of the old seamen, often knitted by the loving hands of their wife while they were away at sea. In response to our admiring inquiries, Dudley told us that it was a birthday present from Joan, his wife, now out of the Island on a visit to her family.

We punted out to 'Taquah' on the moorings with dawn just breaking. There was four of us, Dudley's two longstanding friends George, Tony and myself set for a jaunt down to Chausey for the weekend. 'Taquah' was soon ready to leave the mooring, legs on the foredeck lashed down, sails ready to hoist and the motor checked and running nicely. The bow mooring was slipped and now the stern moorings, Dudley pushed the gearlever into astern and after a few turns of the propeller we moved slowly astern only for the engine to stop and 'Taquah' to stop too. Yes, we were moored by the propeller.

Dudley was determined to free her. Fortunately 'Taquah's' propeller was just exposed at the stern of the hull as it protruded into a cutout on the transom hung rudder. Dudley fairly threw himself over the stern as the crew fended off the yachts around us and held her in place. Only Dudley's legs could be seen as he hung batlike over the aft end of the cockpit alongside 'Taquah's' wheel. At last after about quarter of an hour Dudley had undone the tangled rope and we were free. We pulled her out of the mooring before risking the turning propeller once more.

Dudley was wet from his head to his waist and went down below to change into dry clothes and to towel himself down. We had a pleasant weekend as usual and came back to St Helier on the Sunday afternoon. Dudley went straight home and with Joan away, 'borrowed' her washing machine to put his sodden clothes through the programme, his washing included of course the birthday 'Jersey'.

Now to wash clothes was a fairly new adventure for Dudley and he would not have done it had Joan been at home so there was some excuse for what happened. When the washing machine had finished its programme Dudley opened the door and found all the washing just fine except that he could not find his 'Jersey', there was only a small size one obviously belonging to Michael, his youngest son. Closer examination revealed that it was Dudley's 'Jersey' now several sizes smaller and very thick. On her return Joan soon explained to Dudley about wool and high temperature wash programmes.

We were all quite young, I was in my late twenties, Yvonne was just twenty-one when we saw the 'old man' Bob Kempster, who must have been all of thirty something, struggling to move

Splash And Splot

his Falcon across the mud from where it lay to a better position on the sand. Several of us went to give him a hand and with something like six of us around the boat she began to slither across the black mud towards the clean sand a little way off. Yvonne looked so pretty, she was wearing a white top and neat white shorts and had seized the painter which lay coiled up in the bow. She was tugging this light rope, which must have seen better days, when suddenly it broke.

Long hair and little white outfit not withstanding, Yvonne was rewarded for helping with the Falcon by falling backwards into the mud. Everyone ran to help her up, but the damage had been done she was black from head to foot. The boat was abandoned, someone fetched a nearby hose and we spent the next five minutes cleaning her up! I am sure that most girls would admit that they may have reacted differently, but Yvonne took it all in her stride and was soon changed and back on the beach. By that time we had moved the Falcon and had helped Bob to turn her over so that he could scrub the bottom.

Many years later, I was not very far away from the scene of the above incident, I had been working on some minor defect on 'Blue Raven's' transom when a problem suddenly arose. I had just washed down the transom having finished what I had been doing, my hands were wet and I was standing on a strong beer box on the mud. As I examined the job preparatory to getting off my perch and clearing up, I idly shook my hands to get rid of some of the water and felt my new wedding ring fly off my left hand.

I had no idea in which direction it had gone. I froze and looked down around me at the mud, it was churned up by my sailing boots in every direction. It was impossible to see where the ring may have disappeared. What would Yvonne say, I knew she would be upset as we had chosen the rings carefully together in Gallichan's little jewellery shop in the Royal Square. I stared at the oozing, black mud and carefully lowered myself down onto my knees on the box afraid to stand on the mud lest I trampled the ring deeper into this mess.

Bob Lawrence was close by in 'Bettabob', his motor launch sitting in the cockpit chatting with friends. They were waiting for the tide to float them off for the tide was creeping across the moorings. He told me later that they had wondered what I was doing as I knelt on the box for half-an-hour or more hardly moving. At last I had examined every inch of the surrounding mud and had decided to concentrate on an area to my left as being the most likely direction for the ring to have gone. In all that sea of mud there was just one little muddy hole or indentation different from all the other marks, but no glint of gold. I stood on the mud took a step over to the tiny depression, put one finger into it and lifted out a very muddy ring! I was so relieved.

CANALS AND RIVERS

It is not a best kept secret that, not far from Jersey, just up the river Rance, twelve miles from the fine old walled town of St Malo, lie many miles of beautiful waterways. For those to whom exploring deep into the countryside by boat is a delight, there is a rich prospect of discovering the wildlife and charming villages, towns and the city of Rennes. These rivers and canals are not overused; commercial traffic carried by peniches has long since disappeared and there is not a great number of leisure craft there either. Yet it is free. There are no charges whatsoever and this is locked up in ancient charters given by the French government to the people of Brittany to keep them on side. Similarly, no toll charges are permitted on motorways which pass through the Breton landscape.

It was Napoleon who decided to canalize the rivers of Brittany to assist in the transport of soldiers and materiel. The engineers built many locks and the lovely two storey lock keepers houses. The lock keepers are no longer the war widows of another age, but are often students or men and women who man perhaps three less busy locks with the help of a small car or moped. Time passes slowly by and a pleasant chat with some of this fraternity can often be both amusing and informative.

They all carry mobile phones and if you obtain a list of their telephone numbers this can make your days in the canal run very smoothly. Perhaps you decide to stop in a quiet reach to have lunch and when you are moored to the riverbank you can give the next lock a ring for he will have been informed of your approach by the last lock keeper. This makes things much more 'agreeable' as Monsieur ou Madam can get on with something else while waiting for you.

Need I describe the beauty and tranquillity of a river to you? Be assured that there are the most beautiful tree lined vistas, high granite cliffs and stretches where the fields waving with windswept grasses and crops drift down to the water's edge. Cattle and horses graze contentedly as you ripple past at four or five miles per hour, the required speed on the canals, although it can be faster on the wider more southerly sections. Who wants to hurry? It is beautiful and so relaxing. But I have met yachtsmen who have found it boring and some who only use the canals to traverse Brittany as quickly as possible to avoid making the long sea passage around the rocky western headland. I understand their feelings, but enjoy the sight of kingfishers hurrying from perch to perch along the riverbank and sometimes hovering right beside you to pick some tasty passing morsel from the air or to examine the place beneath the water where a fish awaits his attention.

Yet there are times when the rivers and canals be it the Rance or the Erdre can offer the unwary some minor problems. It was a long time ago when Captain Rory Malkin set forth with Terry Ashborn to spend a pleasant week or two 'up river'. Things had gone well, the weather was kind and they were thoroughly enjoying life aboard Captain Malkin's motorlaunch. Suddenly, as they purred along, there was a loud cracking noise and the craft swung sharply towards the bank and stopped although the engine was still running. The cause of the sudden halt was soon revealed when water rose inside the cabin and pulling back bunks revealed a stake of wood, a small branch of a tree, impaling the hull while water rushed in through a broken plank. With presence of mind, they went astern and struggled to clear the branch then rammed the boat alongside the towpath where the water was shallower. Terry could never explain his next action, but it must have been a reflex for he seized a flare from a locker and fired it there and then deep in the countryside! There was not a huge demand for sea rescue or indeed for river rescue in that neck of the woods and no such assistance would have been forthcoming. However, Terry's rocket now returning to earth and still burning had one dramatic effect which did bring out the farmer and the village too. The rocket set fire to a field of wheat and the ensuing fire and smoke was a sight to behold!

After the fire had been put out, the crew was able to pacify the indignant local populace and to explain their problem. Tractors and farm machinery appeared and the launch was emptied of everything and manhandled onto the towpath. Further assistance poured in over the next few days and soon a good repair was made of the hull, but not before much cider had been drunk and possibly a little calvados too. Terry learned that there had been a local river event quite recently and that the offending stake or 'withy' as they would call it in some parts of England had been a marker on the river. Perhaps a little guilt had played a part in the plentiful assistance so freely given, but again, perhaps not, for the Breton Celt like his Cornish and many other cousins can be a most kindly and feeling friend. The boat was launched again and Captain Malkin and Terry took leave of their many friends with some regret.

Our very first visit to these canals began in the '60s' when we had just acquired 'Dancing Lady', our well-built McGruer cruiser. I had taken the mast down in St Malo and left it with the gentlemen of the 'Sapeur Pompier' from whom I retrieved it later when a bottle of whisky changed hands. As we moved away from the lock gate at the 'barrage' and glided over the still waters of the Rance, we were both thrilled and enchanted. We have hardly lost this feeling since after many visits.

The girls, Alison and Frances were so very young and we arranged our 'Avon' inflatable dinghy for them on the coachroof and turned it into a paddling pool. On some visits we took a babysitter with us and Jean Tozer then Diana Le Bot had a lovely holiday cruising the canals while Yvonne had wonderful assistance from them. Let me tell you of just one small incident among many.

We had reached Rennes and had moored in the city centre on a quiet towpath freshly tarmaced. It was early evening and as the girls prepared themselves for a visit to the city and an evening meal, I stood outside patiently giving them a bit of space in a crowded cabin. I had changed from my sailing gear and I was reasonably presentable. I heard the sound of young English voices approaching and saw two boys of about eighteen walking towards where I was standing. I could hear every word of their clipped Public School accents. Just then they caught sight of me.

"I say. Look there's a chap let's ask him. What's the word for way is it 'route' or 'rue'?" "Oh, just point and say, Ou est la direction pour Redon ou St Malo" They arrived alongside me. "Bon soir, monsieur." And, before I could reply, "Ou est la route pour Redon ou St Malo." I eyed them carefully, they were such genuine youngsters, well dressed in a casual way. I decided to play it straight. "Good evening. Which do you want, Redon or St Malo." They were completely taken aback, to use a lovely nautical phrase. "Oh damn," said the enquiring one, "My first time speaking French to a Frenchman and he turns out to be English!"

It turned out that they were a party of eight boys who had brought canoes from England by train. My two had been sent down to the river to 'recce' the landscape and especially to find out in which direction to paddle their canoes. The 'girls' arrived just then as girls often do when young male voices are heard and we soon learned that they were from Stonyhurst. It was holiday time and one of their teachers was on honeymoon in a village near Redon. The group had decided to call in on him, as a surprise!

The remainder of the party arrived, introductions were made and we took our leave as they set up camp for the night. They had slipped away quietly by morning as we prepared to move off in their wake. Towards the end of a long sunny day we caught up with them at almost our final lock for the day. They were burnt by the sun and their hands were blistered, they were in quite a state. Yvonne had a little queue for treatment on the towpath alongside our boat. Modantis cream was liberally applied, just as Yvonne had done as a young nurse outside the casualty department for all the visitors to Jersey who had overdone the sunshine. In those days she had often stood on a chair in the hospital corridor and handed out tubes of Modantis Cream to a small crowd of sufferers. Now hands were treated and bandaged and it was a sorrowful sight as they stood like little boys waiting for 'Mum' to tend them.

They could row no further so we offered to tow them along the river, an offer which was readily accepted. We tied the canoes in a long string and motored on until we stopped at around seven in the evening. First aid again. I believe they enjoyed the attention of the two girls for Yvonne was in her twenties and very pretty while Diana was sixteen and later became Miss Battle of Flowers. Well, you know what boys are; perhaps they may not have noticed the girls, don't you think!

We nursed the boys along for a few days, while they sported washing lines rigged fore and aft on their canoes. The canoes themselves were wrong for a long trek upriver. They were heavy being made of wood and canvas and too directionally stable requiring considerable effort to make them follow a meandering river. Eventually, after a strong effort, the boys had enough and decided to stop. It was a pity to leave them to return to Rennes, we missed them.

Canals And Rivers

We, that is Yvonne and I, quite often advise newcomers to the canals on lock procedures, which are in truth very simple and on cabin heights above the water, 'tirant d'air'; so essential if you are to pass your boat under low bridges, among other things. Fuel can be a problem and "Do I tip the lock keeper?" and so on and so on. Simple things which experience has taught us can be valuable. For instance, to secure your fenders at the base of the stanchions, not at the top nor on the handrail. We once waited outside a lock for a Guernsey registered motor yacht which had entered before our arrival, to reverse out. When it emerged, we saw that its long stainless steel pulpit had been ripped backwards and upwards with good pieces of fibre glass still attached to the bolts which had once secured it. Fenders which had been secured along the top of the pulpit had become trapped in the substantial wood framing of the lock gate as the yacht entered and with a little speed and the weight of this Guernsey built 'Aquastar' the pulpit fastenings had not stood a chance.

The young owner and his wife, experiencing their first visit to the canals, but now very upset, were determined to hurry back to sea and to home in Guernsey. After a chat, a cup of tea, and a little help they recovered their composure and we used a block and tackle to bend back their badly damaged pulpit so that it rested in approximately its original position. It also helped their recovery, to remind them that their insurance company would be picking up the bill.

There are a good number of hire boats available from the small marina at Guipry – Messac, a village just south of Rennes and others from both Redon and Arzal. These are modern riverboats, well founded and often of a good size, perhaps between thirty and forty feet overall. They are designed to be easy to handle and very tough. They need to be tough!

Not all the 'skippers' who hire them have any knowledge of boat handling especially at close quarters! The boats are 'sans permis' which means that you do not require the usual training and permit to hire one. The crew at the hiring depots do give rudimentary instruction, but it is very limited in both duration and, as you will see, in its effectiveness. I could write a book about this alone.

Cold panic sweeps the wheelhouse as the boat approaches the inviting lock gate, too fast! GO ASTERN....he remembers the words, but too late he bangs the gearlever right through the gate from ahead to astern. No pause to let the propeller come to rest or the gearbox to ruminate over this new command. BANG....the gearbox jumps as the propeller suddenly rotates in the opposite direction, the weight of the boat carries her forward and the helmsman stands spellbound as the pretty bow in front of him, in which he had until recently taken such delight, now investigates the granite of the wall where, some way to one side, the lock gate is situated. BANG....and SHUDDER as the boat is stopped by solid stonework. Perhaps a little fibreglass or black rubber fendering flies noisily past the window. Do we remember even now to take the boat OUT OF ASTERN, possibly not, with further interesting results.

Quite a few 'would be' navigators give up after a day or so of 'adventures'. The most recent occurrence of this was at Dinan in 2007. A Spanish gentleman and his family were aboard a new thirty-two foot riverboat which had been delivered for them from Guipry-Messac so that they could take it up river back to that marina. The Spaniard received the 'normal' instruction and was then cast off into a river flowing at about two knots against him as he made his way so slowly over the current. It was painfully slow because he did not realize that down below, on the beautifully decorated steering console, someone had left the gearlever in a slightly 'ahead' position thereby over-riding his gearlever above on the flyingbridge. The sun was shining, the day was young and a real family adventure lay ahead, a week of pure enjoyment. All this was destroyed as he tried to jockey the boat out of the way of others and ended up with his stern tight against the bank with the rudder broken on the loose boulders and the propeller trying its hardest to refashion a carefully chosen rock. We all got him back to his starting point, but the following day he left by road with his family and their luggage. I expect that the lawyers are still writing to each other.

Brian Slous is a good friend of considerable experience of both the sea and rivers. Several times we hired two of the largest 'Atlantic' class riverboats and took twenty sixteen year old students on a week's canal cruising at the end of the Summer term during what was called, euphemistically, 'Activity Week'. The boys and girls warmed to the experience and all took turns in steering the boats for lengthy periods and other duties. As we approached a lock, boys would swarm up the lock gate to 'assist' Madame, who often enjoyed the fun. I am sure that to this day, thirty years on, many now grown men and women would recall with pleasure their days on the river.

For a change one year, Brian and I decided to move our hiring location and ventured into Burgundy at Laval. On arrival at the quayside, two young Frenchmen who owned the outfit would hear nothing of years of experience, but needs must 'instruct' us both and separately on the ways of boats and rivers. "This is the wheel, M'sieu, you turn it this way to turn right etc...." We were patient and at last having grasped enough of elementary boathandling, the engines were started and the two boats moved out into the river in the hands of our instructors. "This is how you stop." Bang into astern, I winced, and "To turn around in the river...." Apparently this involved charging the bank bow on at speed and then charging the opposite bank stern first, thus bending the rudder mechanism so that it jammed hard over. My instructor now 'lost it', not that he ever had much to lose and began wild gyrations while I stood by anxious not to interfere and still showing every sign of being willing to 'learn', if somewhat perplexed and not a little amused. Enough was enough and eventually I used the back of my hand gently to push him aside and then managed, by judicious use of the ahead and astern thrust on the locked rudder, to regain some measure of control and the quayside. Repairs were made and no further 'instruction' was offered. We enjoyed the boats and had a good time.

"Non, non, M'sieu, par l'avant, pas l'arriere!" The voice rang down from a wooded hillside and I could see no one. Brian had run aground while waiting outside a lock and I had put a line onto the stern of his hireboat to pull him off astern. It did not work. Now a strange disembodied voice was urging me to try something else. I manoeuvred round to the port bow and put a line at right angles to the other boat's bow, went astern with mine and Brian's boat just fell into the deeper water. I presumed that the experienced voice had come from some retired peniche skipper and called out my thanks to him.

Some years later, I was motoring along in a powerful, Dellquay 'Ranger', there was a line of small galvanized steel buoys marking a channel through an abundance of flowering waterlilies. Our good friends Molly and Michael Hubbard were enjoying a holiday with us. There it was, a large, new hireboat showing too much waterline, high and dry on the wrong side of the buoys. We slowed to a stop and hailed the stranded craft. A Frenchman came out of the cabin and I offered to tow him off. To my surprise he refused saying that his friends were coming along behind him in a similar yacht and that they would tow him off, but thank you for the offer. We waved goodbye and motored on.

After some time, perhaps half-an-hour or more, there it was, an identical yacht on the opposite side of the river, equally well stranded. The only difference being that the skipper was in his underpants, covered in mud and attempting to push the bow of the heavy vessel back into deep water! We stopped. Our offer was readily accepted.

He clambered up over the stern of his boat, all the while assisted by his young family on the deck. I motored carefully up to his port side recalling the advice I had once received. Michael followed my instructions and took the hireboat's rope around our forward samson post. I backed away using both engines. The big boat fell back into the river at once and Michael quickly threw back the rope while I moved our boat out of the way. The skipper and his crew were so relieved and grateful.

"We have to hurry," he said, "our friends are away ahead of us." I told him not to worry, that his friends were waiting for him further along the river, waiting to be towed off the mud by him. His face was a picture.

Terry Ashborn became a canal addict and it was on one trip along the canals as far as Redon that an odd accident happened.

Terry and Pam were aboard their Halmatic 8.80 motor sailer and we had just left a lock together with 'Hooky' leading the way. I could see from my position at the wheel of 'Deenie Too', our Fairey Fisherman, that Terry was steering and also busy making an entry in his log and not paying attention to his course up the river. 'Hooky' was about half-a-mile ahead of us when she swung violently to port, heeled to starboard and kicked her stern quite high. Pam was on the starboard side of the deck forward of the cockpit just taking in the scenery when, to my surprise, with the sudden movement of the boat she just took right off and fell into the water a little distance away from the yacht's side. She disappeared completely. I shouted to Yvonne who was down below and pushed the throttle open to get to Pam quickly.

As we neared the site of Pam's disappearance a few moments later, Pam had reappeared and was gasping for breath. We slid up to her in neutral and managed to catch her with the boathook and draw her to our stern. Then we found that despite our combined efforts we could not lift her up the three feet to our deck. Yvonne quickly took a sheet which was lying handy and passed a loop under Pam, who was well-built and soaked through and through and with this we got her to the lifelines and sat her on the narrow edge of the deck to recover. She was exhausted and bleeding a little from her mouth. After a few minutes, she recovered enough to help us get her over the lifelines and into our cockpit where she sat for a while.

Meanwhile, Terry who was obviously quite shocked was standing in his cockpit not far away still fumbling with his lifebuoy which had been almost inaccessible, hidden under his inflatable dinghy carried on the stern. Pam was angry, "Why didn't you do something?" she called over to him. Yvonne took

Pam below for a shower and both boats made their way to the nearby marina at Guipry-Messac. Once tied up, Pam recovered well, but would not rejoin Terry for another hour or two.

The following morning when we stopped for lunch at a neat little log cabin restaurant, Terry raised the matter of the 'log' he had hit. I could not avoid pointing out that the guide to the river in that area warned boat skippers to stay well to the right bank because of rocks in the centre of the river. We heard no more of 'logs' and Terry was, I believe, a little more careful. In truth, Terry had been writing his ship's log or notes, as he usually did and had wandered off course.

No such incident can destroy the beauty and tranquillity of the French canal system. My longest journey along the canals began when my good Guernsey friends, David and Micky Nicolle asked me If I was free to accompany them on a delivery job with a difference. A thirty-eight foot overall motor yacht was to be collected from Cambrills on the Spanish Mediterranean coast, well south of Barcelona, and taken to Paris by way of Sete and the Rhone. It was to be a winter delivery beginning about the end of December. I willingly accepted as I had known David and Micky and their family for many years through sailing. In fact we had first met along the Rance some twenty years before.

The arrangements were made and we travelled south by road in a diesel Mercedes driven by the yacht's owner, Steen. Steen seemed to be a wealthy middle-aged entrepreneur of Danish nationality, but a 'player' on the European stage. He was always striving to find some new enterprise which would make money. His latest 'baby' was a tough canvas air deflector which would when fitted, allow the giant lorries of today to travel more economically. The idea failed eventually because the lorries began to sprout their own glassfibre air deflectors. Steen was accompanied by a lovely young girl of a good French background who could have been his daughter. The Channel Islands 'coven' was a little dismayed when Steen advised us that he and the young girl would accompany us from Cambrills as far as Sete. I think that David and Micky nearly resigned the commission on hearing this.

Cambrills was reached on New Year's Eve and Steen entertained us to dinner in a restaurant of this small Spanish Town. The following morning we set off from the marina in the most perfect weather, warm and calm. David soon noticed that we were only making about ten knots when he expected twelve and this would affect our course planning.

I opened up the engine covers and nestled down beside the twin Ford diesels. I checked various adjustments and noticed that the exhaust fumes trailing behind us were quite black. Not enough air perhaps. David shut down the port engine at my request and I removed the air intake cover. The air filter seemed clean, but I thought that it would be worthwhile starting up without it in place, just to see. As soon as David restarted the engine and pushed the throttle forward the yacht began to turn to starboard and to gather some speed. At David's earnest entreaty I gave the starboard engine the same treatment and we saw the yacht gain two knots and the black exhaust smoke disappeared. This yacht had been cruising along for years with insufficient air to make the diesel fuel burn cleanly. The air filters remained off the engines.

After a night at Barcelona and another at Banyuls we headed for Sete and came into the port late in the evening ahead of an approaching high wind. Fishermens' 'nourrice' or fish holding boxes in great array blocked the charted entrance to Sete and David had to work his way around them. We made the largely unused inner basin and slept well.

Sete was beautiful in the morning light. Fishermen repaired their nets and the whole atmosphere was so tranquil. Steen made arrangements to leave with 'friend' and all three crew members breathed more easily. Steen was no yachtsman and on one occasion I had to sit for a couple of hours with my back to the windspeed indicator in the wheelhouse while engaging Steen in animated conversation so that he would not see the needle heading for twenty knots.

Now a problem arose, Steen had gone, but we could not leave the port and enter the canal system as there was a fishermens strike on and the French CRS, a tough brigade of Gendarmes, would not allow the five electrically controlled bridges which stood in our way to be opened. I went for a walk and by chance dropped into an old chart shop and got into conversation with its owner. I mentioned our problem and he wondered why we did not try the new, as yet unopened, canal entry which debouched into the sea just to the east of the harbour. David decided to give it a try and we took a bearing off the chart and began our run in towards the coast. Nothing! We let the yacht run further in keeping an eye on the depth when, hello, there was an old oildrum with a thick rope tied around it and suddenly, we could see a well camouflaged entrance. We turned into it and so began the most beautiful canal trip you could imagine.

Although cold at times, the weather was perfect and we began to cruise through the beautiful landscape of the Camargue. At times we seemed to be floating on a sheet of glass extending outwards from us for miles in every direction, although actually we were keeping carefully to a well-defined channel. The handsome white horses on other stretches of this canal came across the wet marshland throwing up sheets of spray from their confident hooves as they cantered and turned and flew in the pure joy of freedom. Small collections of cottages, brilliantly coloured in reds and blues and yellows seemed to float alongside us as we passed them by, the winter weather having brought the usual rise in the local water levels.

Avignon with its unfinished bridge and medieval town was delightful and had a little marina mostly frequented by British yachtsmen, some permanently berthed there while others had chosen to winter in this demi-paradise. As we prepared to leave we were earnestly advised to stay on in the manner of the lotus eaters as, "....there was heavy ice on the Rhone further up river...." we were assured that it was dangerous to proceed and that we could damage our yacht. Two men had died just a week or two ago when their vessel had become involved with the ice, we were warned. For good measure we were advised not to have contact with the peniche skippers, that body of professional bargees who navigate the river all their working lives.

To compound our foolishness, I got into conversation with one of these fine sailors and asked him about the ice problem further north and the death of the two men. He was dumbfounded. There was little or no ice and the only accident he had heard about within recent years was when a tractor had been used on the river bank to tow a barge and the barge had taken command and pulled the tractor into the river. No one had been hurt. We did encounter ice a day or two later, it must have been all of perhaps four millimetres thick!

To give full justice to this month long canal journey in the winter of 1989 would require not just a chapter, but a small book on its own. How can I so briefly describe the beauty of the frost clad landscape as we moored up for a whole Sunday deep in the French countryside near a small village, because all the locks were closed. Nothing stirred and we crunched along the frosted lane to the village to enjoy the warmth of the local cafe and its wine.

Darkness fell suddenly in those wintry days and we often moored up in the dark recalling the Prologue from Henry V. 'Now entertain conjecture of a time when stilly murmur and creeping dark hold sway o'er all the earth....' One night, we 'parked' behind an enormous new shedlike building just outside Lyons. The towpath was brilliantly lit and I decided to go for a walk on my own to give David and Micky a bit of space. As I walked along the back of this huge, blank building I emerged into a wide, well-lit space in front of it to find that it was a large supermarket. It was open so I went in and found that due to the wintry weather I was practically on my own inside it. I made a few purchases of presents for my family and wine for the boat. How surprised my companions were when on boarding, I told them what it was. They left the yacht soon to return, loaded down with bags of 'goodies' including some fine wine, as I do recall.

It must have been about 6.30 one dark morning in central France, about two weeks into our 'cruise', when David knocked urgently on my cabin door and shouted for me to come quickly. We were sinking! Water was flooded across the engine room and rising quickly in the light of our torches. The automatic electric pump was not working and the only hand pump was inadequate on this expensive craft. I could not see where the water was coming into the boat, but it was certainly coming in quickly.

An idea hit me. The engine intake pumps were quite big. The water was deep around the sides of the engines as I followed the large, black rubber intake pipe, now well underwater, to the intake valve on the hull. I closed it and using a kitchen knife cut through the rubber pipe close to the valve. David tried that engine and fortunately it started up at once and began to suck the water out of the engine compartment and discharge it into the canal through the exhaust. We soon had a dry engine room and there was the problem; a gland around the starboard propeller shaft had failed and water was gushing past it.

The gland was well hidden below the steel deckplates and so there and then, soaked in cold canal water, without breakfast began the job of getting access to the problem. Hours later, the gland was repacked and the engine room restored to normal including the cut intake pipe. Our client, Steen, had almost lost his yacht through bad maintenance. I found the electric bilge pump. It was well hidden and although big and expensive, it was a mass or very hot rusted metal. The electric motor was seized and was acting as a heater coil very effectively. David had wondered why the batteries were always low despite being charged throughout each day, he had even brought a French electrical engineer aboard to check out the system. Obviously the engineer had missed this well hidden fault.

Canals And Rivers

We cruised on through the most beautiful countryside being required to take the most easterly canal route because of work being done on the Midi and other canals. I was pleased as it meant that we came up through the River Marne, the scene of much fierce fighting during the first world war. I even found a French 1914–1918 helmet rusting quietly in the steep riverbank. The gentle undulating hills of the Champagne district with well-known vineyards advertising their acreage in Hollywood style letters several feet high.

Late one afternoon, just as it was becoming dark, we came upon the entrance to a tunnel. Clear instructions on a panel suggested that the tunnel was only wide enough for one boat to pass through at a time. We would have to wait until M'sieu the Chef du Tonnel gave us the word to go. Traffic lights were positioned at the tunnel entrance ready for each skipper to observe. It was all very fine, but there was no 'Chef', in fact no one at all. We waited and at last decided to take a chance and to proceed into the dark cavern of the entrance. By now it was pitch dark and even darker inside the tunnel.

The yacht had a heavy searchlight which we had to take down from its position above the 'bridge' as it was too high to pass under some bridges. Now I mounted the searchlight on my shoulder and standing in the bow shone the light along the narrow way made even narrower by a rickety wooden walkway along the lefthand side of the tunnel. The roof of the tunnel was a low arch cut out of the solid rock and it stretched on and on before me. An hour at four knots passed and Micky brought me a cup of hot chocolate and gallantly offered to take a 'turn' with the heavy light, but I knew it was too much for her to hold. Two hours later, with no mishaps we emerged from this enormous tunnel and moored up in the dead of the night and fell into our bunks after a good hot meal thoughtfully prepared by Micky.

It was not long after this 'adventure' that Micky tore a tendon in her thigh. It happened so suddenly. There had been some rain and we entered a strange lock where the internal walls sloped backwards at a strong angle making it difficult to step off the moored yacht and onto the wet lockside. Micky always 'pulled her weight' and as ever made to leave the side of the boat and because of the distance to the granite paved lock edge she turned around facing the hull and reached out backwards with her foot and pushed herself off the boat.

I was at the bow on the lock itself, David was aboard and the lock keeper was well astern of the boat operating his sluicegates. Suddenly I heard Micky call out and there she was collapsed into a large puddle and crying out in agony; the stretch and awkward push had caused her left leg to collapse as the tendon tore within her thigh. I have been told that a torn muscle or tendon is very painful and this was evident. I rushed to her and could see immediately that we would have to get her aboard. The lock procedure was stopped and David and I had the deck of the yacht brought level with the quayside. Then by using the stern bathing platform we got Micky on to the yacht and into the stateroom.

The extreme pain caused Micky to pass out. We tried everything to ease her discomfort and gently sailed downriver until we could moor up near a bridge in a small town. I soon found a surgery and the good doctor came to the boat as soon as he had seen one or two patients. It was he who diagnosed the problem, as up to then David and I had no idea what it was. He gave Micky some pain relieving drugs and a prescription and was loathe to make any charge for his services, but David insisted.

It was a sadly depleted crew who now took our 'ship' up to Paris Micky had always been around helping and making refreshments, a beautiful and lively girl, now she was being very good about her problem. She could not walk and David helped her when she had to move. Sometimes the pain of moving caused her to faint making David and I think that hospitalisation was the only option. Micky wanted to get home to Guernsey and so we plodded on and eventually entered the huge lock in central Paris, the 'Arsenale' It had indeed been Napoleon's Arsenal where barges loaded with munitions from the French factories supplied the country with the weapons of war.

But now it was a peaceful leisure centre with many permanently berthed yachts and a good yacht club. The entrance to the 'Arsenale' had been well concealed behind a giant hoarding of some sort and was controlled by a television monitor and a rasping mechanical French voice. It worked and in we went, the end of a month's winter sailing which I will never forget, all thanks to my good Guernsey friends, David and Micky Nicolle. We taxied Micky to the Charles de Gaulle airport and wheelchaired her around, still in great pain. At last we took off and dropped into Jersey en route for Guernsey when I took my leave. David and Micky were wonderful companions, I don't think in a month of canal cruising we said a cross word, despite one or two tribulations.

David's father had been the harbourmaster of Guernsey and David himself gave up a career as a science teacher to run his own Sailing School aboard his lovely forty-two foot yacht

'Zephyr'. His experience was of the sort that he used to train and examine not only budding Yachtmasters, but also the Captains of Cross Channel ferries in the difficult arts of navigation in the rockbound Channel Islands waters. We have never lost touch and remain good friends to this day.

As I write more stories enter my thoughts, there have been so many. However, I have detained you long enough and perhaps there could be another book in all of them. Until then should it happen, Good Sailing.

Glossary

ABACK   The wind fills the back or wrong side of the sails. Yacht stops, can be forced over onto its side.

BERMUDAN SAIL   A mainsail of triangular shape.

BLOCK   Often called a 'pulley' by landlubbers. A well crafted grooved wheel (sheave) held between sides or cheeks which changes the direction of a rope passing through it. They can have several sheaves within them in different arrangements and can be of many different materials. Expensive

BOSUN'S CHAIR   A secure canvas or wooden seat which can be hauled up a mast to allow repairs all alterations to be made in relative safety.

CANOE STERN   Many boats have a flat or curved stern, a canoe stern is when the boat finishes like the bow with the sides coming together like a canoe.

CENTREPLATE   A type of keel of wood or metal which slides down or is hinged to resist the sideways movement of a yacht caused by the pressure of the wind.

CLOSE TO THE WIND   A yacht cannot sail directly into the wind, but may sail within up to 40 degrees of the wind. Sail closer than this and the sails will shake and all forward movement will stop.

COME ABOUT   To turn a yacht from its present course into the wind, through the eye of the wind onto another heading. This will cause the sails to be set on the opposite side of the yacht.

CRADLE   A wooden structure which supports a yacht when it is dried out or ashore.

CUDDY   A small shelter often in the bow of a small craft.

DOWNWIND   Any direction away from the wind.

FLYING BRIDGE   A raised steering position usually on the roof of a motoryacht.

GAFF SAIL   A squarish mainsail unlike the triangular bermudan mainsail.

GUNNEL   The top edge of a boat's side, usually well built up to protect the side and rounded to make it kind to ropes and bodies.

GLASS   Relating to a yacht or boat refers to its fibreglass construction of layers of resin and fibreglass mat.

GYBE   To turn a yacht away from the eye of the wind until the mainsail boom swings across and the sails are set on the other side of the yacht. An accidental gybe can be dangerous to the crew and the yacht.

GYBE HO   A warning call given by the helmsman when he is turning a yacht round away from the wind on the opposite point of sailing. The heavy mainsail boom may come across the deck and must be well controlled to avoid accidents and injury.

HALLIARD   Ropes which haul sails towards the head of the mast.

HEAVE TO   By setting a jib to interfere with the flow of air across the mainsail a yacht will almost stop and remain quietly head to wind.

LEE HO   I thought that someone would ask about this one! A warning call given by the helmsman when he is turning a yacht through the eye of the wind. It tells everyone to be ready at sheets and winches and most of all to take care as the yacht heels over on the opposite side.

LEGS   Two supports of wood or metal which prevent a yacht from falling over as she dries out on a beach. I could write a chapter about these items.

MAROON   An explosive warning device used by the lifeboat service which goes off with a distinctive very loud bang to alert lifeboatmen wherever they are to an imminent launch of the lifeboat.

OFF THE WIND   A pleasant experience. The yacht is sailing across the wind which is blowing directly over her side. The yacht sails easily and quickly.

ONE DESIGN   Racing yachts compete under handicap rules to allow everyone to compete fairly. A 'One Design' class of yacht is one of a group of absolutely identical craft. Whichever crosses the finishing line first is the winner.

PONTOON   A floating walkway which provides mooring points for yachts where they may sometimes remain afloat as in a marina. They often provide water and electricity.

REACHING   A point of sailing across the wind when sails are eased off.

REEF   To reduce the area of a sail when it is too big for the prevailing conditions

SCHOONER   A two masted sailing boat in which, unusually, the after mast is taller than the foremast.

SHEET   A rope which is used to control a sail whether it is a jib or mainsail.

STROP   A piece or rope which is made up to form a grip or to secure some item.

SWING   To 'swing' a compass is to turn a boat through 360 degrees while moored and to check the accuracy of the compass against bearings and a standard compass. Metal parts aboard a yacht can cause serious inaccuracies. A card showing problems is then drawn up to provide the crew with corrections for all bearings.

TACK   Sailing craft cannot sail directly into the wind. The laws of physics do not allow this. They must 'tack' to sail a course directly towards the wind. This means zigzagging to achieve slow progress directly into the wind.

THWART A strong plank of wood which lies horizontally across a small boat to strengthen her and to form a useful seat.

TRANSIT   Of great use when navigating close to the shore is a line formed by any two objects such as a lighthouse and a prominent building. They may be picked out in sailing notes or by studying a chart to provide a safe channel past dangers.

TRANSOM   The flat or curved stern of a boat. They are of many shapes and sizes and may have a rudder fastened to them or hold steps. A study in themselves.

WATER   Not for drinking or sailing upon. A racing call when another yacht is forcing your boat off its course when you have right of way.

WINDWARD   A direction directly towards the wind. Usually more difficult to attain under sail.

YARD   It can mean a boom across a mast on a square rigged ship which carries a square sail. 'Yard is also short for shipyard.

About the Author

LEO HARRIS is the successful author of two books 'A Boy Remembers' and 'Boys Remember More' which tell of life during the German Occupation of Jersey. Now he turns to his experience of sailing in the sea around the Channel Islands. He vividly recounts the events and stories he has gathered or experienced over more than fifty years.

He is an experienced lecturer, frequently booked to give talks aboard cruise ships and at other functions. His approach to sailing is reminiscent of his previous books, in turn humourous and serious, carrying the reader forward apace into his writing.

Leo has participated in many aspects of yachting including boat building, racing, delivery and assisting in the running of a major yacht club. He became the Commodore of St Helier Yacht Club in 1980 and still continues to sail a small yacht and keeps a French-built river boat on the River Rance.

Yvonne and Leo have enjoyed over fifty years of sailing together and not quite as long of a very happy marriage. Their children Alison and Frances now have their own families so that Yvonne and Leo enjoy many good times with Peter, Alison's husband and with Ben, Merry, Harry, Laurence and Curtis.

Yvonne: *Who said girls can't build boats?*

ISBN 1-903469-02-3   ISBN 1-903469-05-8

Leo Harris has previously had two very successful books published about his experiences during the German Occupation. They are available from leading book shops or by contacting the publishers on:
Tel: (01534) 860806 Fax: (01534) 860811
e-mail:sales@channelislandpublishing.com